New *Life* in the BOARDING HOUSE

New *Life* in the
BOARDING
HOUSE

the renovation of a
heart and mind

Greg R. Elliott

NEW LIFE IN THE BOARDING HOUSE
Copyright © 2014 by Greg R. Elliott

Unless otherwise indicated, all Scripture quotations are taken from the Holy Bible, New Living Translation, copyright ©1996, 2004, 2007 by Tyndale House Foundation. Used by permission of Tyndale House Publishers, Inc., Carol Stream, Illinois 60188. All rights reserved. Scripture quotations marked KJV are taken from the Holy Bible, King James Version, which is in the public domain.

Citation for Dr. Seuss quotation: Geisel, Theodore. *The Cat in the Hat* (New York, NY: Random House, 1957), p. 55.

Printed in Canada

ISBN: 978-1-4866-0512-5

Word Alive Press
131 Cordite Road, Winnipeg, MB R3W 1S1
www.wordalivepress.ca

WORD ALIVE
—P R E S S—

MIX
Paper from
responsible sources
FSC
www.fsc.org   FSC® C016245

Cataloguing in Publication information may be obtained through Library and Archives Canada

Additional books available at
NewLifeintheBoardingHouse@gmail.com
https://greatcanadianauthors.com
and Indigo / Chapters /Amazon

To my two-shall-be-one
my three and their three who made six
and my eight who made sixteen

A DIY Bible experience
… for anyone who needs a new way to do life
… and those who don't think a new life is possible.

An experience retold, illustrating the step-by-step renovation
of an angry, doubt-filled mind and wounded heart.

In order to get the full benefit of understanding and to establish a comparison point, it is recommended to first read the Scripture verses mentioned at the beginning of each chapter.

Working with the
contractor mentioned in
this book will change your life.

Contents

The Boarding House

introduction to virtual house, visitor at the door

1 THESSALONIANS 5:19–20, MATTHEW 18:19–20

This is my third time here alone. It's late at night and I'm sitting in my favourite old armchair again. I am doing this because a friend said I should try it and my first time doing it left me almost speechless. I have read the first verses listed for today from the paperback Bible and as a result, three questions appear on the whiteboard of my mind—*Who or what is the Holy Spirit and how can you ignore or stifle it? What does this have to do with me?*

As in the first time, a mental image appears. Percussion instruments roll and a theatre curtain parts, revealing the image of an elaborate three-storey house from which emanates sounds of boisterous activity and disorder.

Interior lights proclaim themselves from each of the many uncovered windows. Porches, dormers, turrets, and cupolas protrude from the central structure. Thick clumps of grass, connected by bare patches of hard soil, form the base of the tableau, dotted by discarded, forgotten objects and a sprinkling of sparse flowers. A slightly askew plumber's pipe connects a small sign— reading, "Boarding House"—to a patch of grass at the base of the porch steps. The worn window casements, railings, and gingerbread fretwork interrupt the lines of the pale plank siding. A complicated maze of sagging rain gutters and disjointed down pipes define the corners of the building. Paint flakes speckle the deteriorating bargeboard adornments. A droning, dripping air conditioner juts precariously over a window ledge.

Antiquated lightning rods, with their porcelain orbs and copper lines, project from the ridges of each dormer. Ornately crafted finials and iron railings encrusted with rust frame the patchwork roof like a lop-sided crown. The blue-grey sky betrays the passing of a recent rainstorm.

The detail of this image astounds me. It is meticulously crafted, creating in me a feeling of familiarity, though I'm certain I have never seen it before. This incredible virtual scene is even more graphic than the experience of being shoved.

Amazement, curiosity, and tickling anticipation tease me forward from my comfortable seat of logic. I don't understand what is going on but I want to. Whatever it is, it has filled me with wonder and an indefinable sense of goodness. I want this to continue!

What's next?

This mental imaging thing has me amazed and that house has me really curious. I decide to read the second set of verses. This one is written by a follower of Jesus named Matthew. In these verses, Matthew retells some of the lessons Jesus taught to his disciples in the city of Capernaum.

This particular excerpt is about people gathering and agreeing on what they should ask God for in their prayers. Jesus states emphatically that, should they do this, whatever they ask will be done. He expands this incredible statement by saying that whenever a few people gather together, he will be present with them because of their belief in him.

These claims challenge me to understand how such doings are possible, but they don't immediately promise any enlightenment to the old boarding house. Despite my puzzlement, I experience tingles of anticipation as if something is about to happen.

Sure enough, the image of the house pops up in front of me again. I see it from the perspective of the walkway leading up to the front porch. I can hear sounds coming from inside the house as I move towards the door. With concentration, the cacophony separates into its myriad components of radio chatter, conversation, music, kitchen clatter, vocal exclamations, foot-stomping laughter (both hearty and shrill), electrical appliances labouring, cordless tools whining, doors slamming, floors creaking, a clock ticking, a smoke alarm bleeping, fans whirring, fists pounding, hands slapping, and phones ringing. I'm getting agitated as the noise rattles in my eardrums.

Who would want to reside in such a disharmonious dwelling? I find myself entering this virtual image and standing on the worn plank porch, looking for some indication of my next move. To one side of the doorframe, above the flyer-stuffed mailbox, is a small doorbell button, its weak light stuttering intermittently. To my utter astonishment, its marred brass plate has *my* name engraved on its darkly oxidized surface.

After a few moments of speechless pause, spent futilely groping for some understanding of this scene, I yield to a subconscious coaxing that gives me permission to enter.

Gingerly, I cross the threshold into the unmistakable source of the clamorous sounds. The bustling scene is like the loading platform in a large busy bus terminal. Electing to anchor myself—initially, at least—in the relative safety of the small entry hall, I attempt to assess the chaos before me.

Immediately in front of me is a staircase cluttered with obstacles disturbed by the constant jostling of people moving up and down. Individuals cross closely in front of me, interrupting my view of the stairs. Some notice me, while others appear to be unaware of my presence—but no one stops. Gilded baroque frames hold pictures on the wall, and below them a frail-legged table burdened with indistinguishable objects trembles from the hurried movement of people passing by.

Various expletives and epithets of disagreement shoot out from the many corners of the house. They reverberate against other discordant sounds arising from unseen activity. A television set and a radio combat each other as prattling voices and slamming doors battle in a futile effort to be heard above one another, adding to the aberrant symphony.

Again, I recognize this discordant place, yet I also know I've never seen it before. Apprehension pours its icy chill over my shoulders. Suddenly, the bleat of a doorbell forces a flush of alarm through my body.

Turning, I notice for the first time the many locks, night chains, and slide bolts installed on the door. How is it possible for them to have been reset since my entry only moments ago? The doorbell rings loudly, insisting on being noticed. I shuffle to one side, expecting someone from this raucous party to come in response to its summons.

No one comes. Again the bell rings. I watch the continuum of people passing through the hallway. They are oblivious to this new solitary note in the symphony; the existing decibel level swallows it. The bell rings again. My ears try to fit it into this now wrenchingly familiar orchestra of noise and tension.

I will ignore the bell—it has nothing to do with me. Or does it? I remember the nameplate on the doorbell. Immediately, a mix of certainty and trepidation catches up with me. I think I know who is pushing the button, but I'm afraid of opening the door to find out why he's come.

After yet another intrusive ring, I scramble to undo the locks. There are an absurd number of them. Why? Finally, I come to the last latch, this one with a longer chain than the others. I choose to leave it fastened while opening the door. I need to see who's there, but I don't want to risk permitting access before knowing for sure.

My first furtive look through the narrow opening confirms my hunch. It is, indeed, the crisp image of a man in a white shirt. His face and eyes radiate with a compassion that saturates my being. It is Jesus, the Christ.

Until this moment, in which my entire life is suspended in serene motionlessness, I have only glimpsed him from a distance, as in a game of hide-and-seek among the trees. His presence now floods over me and the heaviness within me floats away. The sense of concord radiating from him extinguishes my awareness of the bedlam in this house. Time seems to stop as I stare at this man.

As he smiles, words form in my mind that I'm sure are from the Bible: *"I am come that [you] might have life, and that [you] might have it more abundantly"* (John 10:10, KJV).

Standing there, my entire body feels like it is being filled to overflowing with a warm liquid, full in body and excruciating in its wholesomeness. There is nothing to see, but every atom of my being feels different at this moment. A vital part of me that was missing is for some reason restored. Thoughts coming from deep within my chest tell me this is pure, unconditional love. I want it to always be there.

"Come to me, all of you who are weary and carry heaven burdens, and I will give you rest" (Matthew 11:28). These words from Jesus are familiar because I have read them before on roadside signs.

Yes. I cry aloud, tears and a trembling chin accompanying my words. Yes, I want to be rid of the joyless weight that has been suffocating my life. What do I have to do? *"Because they love me, my Father will love them, and I will love them. And I will reveal myself to each one of them"* (John 14:21).

At that moment, a tiny seed hidden deep within me demands an explosive release from the dark tomb of rubble in my soul. It is a love that recognizes the voice calling to me. It is the first time I've ever felt the capacity to love anyone in spite of my many previous professions of it.

Though I do not personally know this man who stands on the porch before me, I'm pretty sure he is the one whom preachers and roadside signs claim loves us so much that he willingly suffered the unjust fear, pain, and indignity of death so that none of us will be punished for our wrongdoings.

Comprehension of that statement still eludes my logic, but its truth is illuminated and understood by the love now bubbling and rushing within me.

"I will send you the Counsellor—the Spirit of truth. He will come to you from the Father and will tell you all about me" (John 15:26).

Yes. Though I don't really understand how it is possible, I just want to say, "Yes, come in, come in."

My invitation is followed by a sudden consciousness of no longer being alone. It feels like my Boarding House has a new boarder. I turn but can see no one else here. I look back towards the door. A warmth envelops me.

"I am with you always."

How I can hear words when there is no one else in the room?

But before I go any further with this story, let me go back a couple of days to explain—as best I can—what is happening.

The Me I No Longer Want to Be

desperation, a pastor and a BBQ

I was white-knuckling along life's expressway without knowing where it was going or understanding why I was on it. Though surrounded by a loving spouse, beautiful children, and genuine friends, a gnawing sense of emptiness and angry detachment lurked within me. My response to everything was negative and very little felt like fun anymore. It seems it has always been this way. As a little guy, I figured out my father didn't like me but I didn't know why. I hid in fear when he started verbal and physical fights with my mother and cried often because I couldn't protect her. I was very unsure of myself and had few friends in school. Confrontations with just about everybody accompanied me through high school and blew up my dream of going to university.

Everything was always a struggle, nothing seemed to work for me. I didn't understand what was wrong. Most days had me feeling confused, trapped and combative. There was no one I trusted enough to talk to about it all but I was too embarrassed to tell anyone what I was feeling anyway.

These cancerous emotions focused sharply one painful night when I decided to resolve the rejection, fear, and anger that characterized the space between my father and me and tainted everything else in my life. Emotionally, I crossed a line that night. Thankfully, my impulsive intention was thwarted and the gun remained in its rack.

The next day, after witnessing my latest outburst, a co-worker suggested that I call a church pastor for help. I wanted to laugh, but couldn't. I didn't go to church—I didn't have a pastor.

I was breaking into an angry rampage at someone or something almost daily. Walls, cars, people and almost anything else that crossed my line of sight was a potential target for my punches. I couldn't sleep at night and a cold chill penetrated my shoulders most days. Life just wasn't fair. I wanted to escape. What could a pastor do for me?.

An uncharacteristic flash of clarity came to me one night as I read a popular Dr. Seuss story to my children.

> *"This mess is so big*
> *So deep and so tall,*
> *We cannot pick it up.*
> *There is no way at all."*

These words, sputtered by the fish in Dr. Seuss' well-known *The Cat in the Hat*, accurately express the disarray I felt inside me—in my thoughts. If you could see it, my inner life would look like a tired old house in a rundown neighbourhood. The yard messy, parts and pieces missing or broken, and paint peeling off the walls. There was a long list of things that weren't right. It should either be fixed or demolished.

"You need to talk to a pastor!" My co-worker was trying to help, but he only added to my sense of hopelessness. His words gave me no comfort. I was full of fear and agitation and unable to find comfort or humour in anything. There were times when I wondered if I was experiencing a mental breakdown, but psychiatrists say that in such a crisis a person would experience detachment from reality and be unable to think clearly about their situation. As much as I wanted to be detached from the reality of this emotional pain and be unable to think about my fear and anger, I couldn't get free from either of them. Nothing seemed right to me—in the world, in the people around me, and in myself. If there *was* a God maybe he was angry with me. I felt separated from everything and everyone. It wasn't a pastor I needed but a new life.

Why do people go to church? I wondered. *What do they find in the Bible?*

Everything around me—institutions, television, businesses, and educators—taught and supported scientific explanations for our existence. I hadn't bumped into any credible witnesses to the contrary, so I had always gone along with the common opinion that there was no God. Most people I knew seemed to have no idea what the Bible really is or what to do with it. If there was no God, then it must be a storybook for people with feeble hearts and similar minds.

I'd heard some of the stories of the Bible and about Jesus. Even as a kid dragged off to Sunday school, I found it hard to believe much of what my teachers told us. The older I got, the more I doubted those stories.

"You need to talk to a pastor!" I tried to dismiss my co-worker's words, but they wouldn't leave. Neither could I dismiss my unsettled state of mind. A couple of days later my desperation finally drove me to a church and the office of the pastor. We talked for a while, I don't remember about what, and as I left he asked me to go with him to what he called a men's group barbeque. I didn't have a better idea to get rid of the mess inside me so a few days later found me eating burgers with a bunch of guys I didn't know. They weren't what I expected—they seemed pretty ordinary. They laughed, joked and told stories about their work, sports and families. There was also some animated discussion about some stuff they were reading in the Bible that caught my ear.

Later, at home, curious about what those guys were talking about, I dug through a bookcase for a book given to me a long time ago. It was still there—an unopened paperback edition of the Bible titled *The Way*. That's what I was looking for—the way out of the mess I'm in. I started flipping pages, finally settling on a page titled John 14.

After reading for only a couple of minutes, I found my thought life abruptly and roughly shoved off the expressway I've been barrelling down and into a calm stillness.

Shoved?

Yes, I say I was "shoved," and not only that, I could also see and recognize my assailant, though I now realize I saw it all through my "heart", not the cardiovascular pump that dislikes cholesterol B, but the heart through which we are tempted to dream by the first whiff of spring in the air.

Practically everyone has seen images of this guy that shoved me. In his trademark image, he is usually pictured wearing a long white mid-eastern style shirt and standing in a circle of sheep holding a lamb while a peculiar neon yellow glow surrounds his head and highlights the sad look on his face. Versions of it can be seen on Christmas cards and in church windows. I wonder why he always looks so sad. Anyway, this is the same guy who shoved me.

In the flurry of action, there was no time to figure out what was going on. A sense of panic vapourized my characteristic defensive response of anger. How can this be happening? Am I suffering a mental breakdown? This guy doesn't really exist, does he?

I admit recognizing the guy in the white shirt—sort of. I have heard about him all my life, in one way or another. But isn't he like Santa Claus? Aren't you supposed to realize about the time you quit your paper route that boys and girls are different? That Santa Claus is really your father? That the Easter Bunny never laid a chocolate egg in its life and that this whole God story is just another line told by adults to stop you from having fun?

It had to be a thing parents used before child psychology was invented— "Santa won't bring any presents if you don't behave. The Tooth Fairy won't leave any money if you create a fuss at the dentist. Your face is going to freeze like that if you don't stop frowning." It puzzled me, though, how my father often called Jesus' name from the workshop, usually right after something crashed to the floor. Did that mean Jesus was real? Was he being asked for help, or was he being blamed for what happened? I had never heard of anyone who actually had seen God or Jesus so I concluded my father was simply a victim of his own trickery. Besides, if he did know Jesus then why did he treat my mother the way he did? Why didn't he want to spend time with me? What about the way he always dismissed the things I did or said? I decided God couldn't be real.

As I got older, I often saw or heard references to this so-called creator of everything, however the people making the references were rarely those I would choose as my role models. They were always at the sidelines, calling out rules, cautioning my actions, never being involved in the fun around them. Often their comments were about right and wrong and threats of God's judgment. My observation of their lives provided nothing to attract me, and sometimes they confused me by the difference I saw between what they said and what they did. I decided they were people who were unable to live without some kind of crutch. They were living a delusion. I believed in myself. I didn't need this God stuff for my strength.

A couple of times when things were particularly rough, I secretively tried asking this God for help but nothing happened, confirming for me that it was all just a lot of nonsense.

As I headed off into young adulthood, I was attracted by the excitement in the long string of interesting people, events and promising opportunities in the parade of life I saw all around me. Maybe there I could find acceptance and love. I wanted to be a part of this parade of promises that claimed it could fix the holes in me and fulfill my dreams. So I joined it and enthusiastically followed along.

As the years went by though, it became apparent this parade couldn't make good on most of its promises, and in fact delivered more discouragement than dreams. The colour and fun became more like a mask for pain. I didn't like who I had become nor how those "holes" inside of me always caused hurt for the people around me. Eventually I wanted out.

That is where I was at when this surreal encounter took place. My logic groaned in protest at the thought that it was possible, yet I couldn't deny it. This guy's confident serenity clearly indicated that he knew exactly who he was, and he knew exactly who I was. If this guy in the white shirt *was* real—then God must be as well. This thought, for some inexplicable reason, planted the hope in my head that a new "me" was possible. I hadn't felt hope for a very long time and this tiny taste left me thirsty for more.

As crazy as it sounds, I needed to see if I could get this unreal experience to happen again.

I didn't know how to start so I grabbed the paperback Bible again and a little daily reading guide a friend gave me a long time ago in the hope that it would help me. He explained it was intended to guide a person through the Bible and contained a suggested short selection to read for each day of the year. It somehow survived my intention to throw it out. He also suggested at the time that I should have a notebook with me and write down whatever thoughts I had as I read the verses, so I did that too.

Plunked into a chair, I looked up the selection for the day, finally found it in the Bible and then read it. I quickly discovered the experience *could* happen again and in fact *did* happen many more times. The pages that follow tell the story as I recorded it in the note books after each encounter.

The Mad Parade
the search for a peaceful mind and hope

LUKE 19:1–10

'm back home from that barbeque, the kids are in bed and all is quiet. I have an unused paperback Bible with me and a book that lists daily Bible readings. The way those guys were talking about the Bible has stirred something in me.

Yet, how can this Bible contain anything relevant? Its contents are centuries old. You can't trust the words written in last night's newspaper to be truthful or accurate. How can these old, many-times-translated writings have anything dependable in them?

Not knowing exactly what to do next, I close my eyes and stammer some awkward words into the air to the effect that I need help. Immediately there is a flash of movement as a man in white shoves me—hard. I'm still physically in my chair but mentally I feel like I have landed somewhere different. The lighting is very dim lighting and I am alone. I am also frightened.

A cold, sharp laugh from somewhere within stings me as I ask, "What's the matter wimp, can't you take it? Shape up and get a grip. This is what life is. There's nothing else but your own strength so make it happen the way you want. Quit this nonsense of thinking you can change."

A fleeting image of the guy in white flashes back into my mind. A shiver of anticipation rushes through me.

"Are you still here?" I ask aloud, dubiously.

"I am."

There is no one else in the room yet I hear spoken words. My thoughts bounce back to the Bible in my hands. I can't believe I'm actually going to read it. Why am I doing this? I want some real answers, some relief from all the crazy thoughts that ricochet through my head as I spend hours trying to fall asleep at night and struggle through each day.

Silence and darkness. My shoulders feel cold again.

A distant clatter scratches across the silence.

"You must come to me through my word, and it is in that Bible."

The grammar seems a little odd, but remembering the guy in the white shirt and hearing these words from nowhere incline me to read. I don't want to read any silly old stories but I'm not willing to run the risk of asking if I have any other choice. The little guide book indicated that the part to read on this date is Luke, chapter 19. I open the paperback Bible and flip through the pages until I find the title "Luke." Thankfully, no one can see what I'm doing. I read the first ten verses in chapter 19.

The story I find there is about a little guy who hoisted himself up onto the branch of a tree hanging above a gathered crowd and over a road to get a better look at Jesus as he passed by. It seems like he just wanted to watch the activity without getting involved. I appreciate his observation post and find myself mentally sitting beside him.

His name was Zacchaeus. It reminds me of all those other strange names I had so much trouble pronouncing years ago as a kid in Sunday school. It was embarrassing, trying to read those verses in front of a class with all the guys stifling snorts and the girls rolling their eyes in that universal sign language for "what a nerd." Add all the "thys" and "thous" and "thines" and "blesseths" and it is easy to see why we resisted efforts by adult types to read that book. Anyway, old remembrances aside, I think old Zack here had the right idea.

That is, until the point when Jesus, the focus of this large crowd and procession, unexpectedly stopped in his tracks, looked right up at Zack, and said, "I want to talk to you later."

Zack wasn't expecting that, nor was I. The story continued, however, to a super ending—or should I say, a beginning? Either way, I find myself wishing it could be my story.

Zap! Ever been told to be careful what you wish for because it might come true? I never believed it—until this moment. The voice of the guy in the white shirt is right there again.

"It *is* your story."

I mentally wiggle out a little further on the branch. I'll watch from here for a while and see what happens next. Zacchaeus just grins at me and, with a sparkle in his wink, gently pokes me with his elbow.

The extraordinary imagery fades and I find myself thinking about parades.

I have loved parades all my life. Most parades are happy celebrations with exuberant displays of music, costumes, clowns, dancers and decorated vehicles. The elaborate floats are designed to amuse and dazzle us, lifting our thoughts above the routine or troubling circumstances of our daily lives.

But what happens if the parade includes all the realities we want to escape from?

A lot of bad things can happen in our personal lives and in the world that hurt or disrupt our sense of being. We make mistakes that result in regret or guilt, sometimes both. We can be robbed of our capacity to be happy and enjoy life. When you are at your lowest, life can appear to be a hopeless parade of madness.

The parade that attracted me years ago has not been the happy parade I expected. Pain, disappointment, disease, sorrow, emptiness, addiction, waste, busyness, threats, injustice, sickness, hopelessness, anger, gossip, infidelity, frustration, cheating, jealousy, fear, selfishness, loneliness, hunger, regret, broken promises, violence, temptation, war, suicide, murder, poverty, lies, divorce, abductions, prostitution, disobedience, abuse—these are some of the parade floats I can see. But where are the clowns? Where are the balloons and tossed candies? Is there a jolly guy in a red suit at the end? *Is* there an end to this parade?

I recoil at the sight of this parade and feel emotionally sore as I think about it. Sure, there are pockets of fun and laughter and meaning but when I'm being jostled along in the midst of the clamour, those good moments are difficult to see or hear and seem impossible to hold onto.

I want out but I don't know how to do it. This parade of life has a way of dragging you back in. You protest. If you have to be tired, lonely, confused, hurt, or just plain angry, you should at least be able to do it in your own way. You don't want to go back, but you are unable to remain at the curb. Is it just me that feels this way?

Questions daily jostle and elbow their way around in my mind.

Is there really a future worth working towards? Are abortion clinics wrong or not? Will my kids be safe? Are there going to be more terrorist attacks? Are we destroying the environment? How can we stop the destruction from addictions? Why do people want to fight and kill each other? Why are there so many starving people in the world? Why are so many leaders morally and ethically bankrupt?

Why do cheaters always win? Why do some people have so much while others have so little? Why are children massacred in a classroom by some emotionally disturbed person with a gun? Why do church ministers molest innocent youth, have affairs with prostitutes, and fraudulently take money from trusting people? Why doesn't my father like me? If there is a God, why is there so much hurt? Why doesn't he do something?

There are answers for these questions in the parade but can I trust them?

Jailbird
first insight into imprisonment and hope

GALATIANS 4:6–7

It's the same night but a little later and I'm still feeling raw from thinking about the parade. I'm feeling locked in, wanting to escape again. I go back to my books and pick another reading.

I finally find the passage—Galatians 4:6–7—and words about slavery and freedom appear before me from a book with a name out of a space movie. There are also some words I don't understand about God's Spirit being put in my heart, but I admit that I'm interested in the part about my freedom. These words talk about freedom from slavery because of the Spirit. But no sooner than the reading starts, it's over.

Freedom? Slavery? The words ring true, but what exactly is holding me captive?

My thoughts start lightly as I think of the financial demands that pin me down. They move on to the feeling of restraint by the physical and emotional drain of my work—driven to seek perfection and coping with demanding deadlines. I think of how I am trapped by other people's expectations of me and my own impatience. Self-doubts, fuelled by my failures and my father's voice also hold me prisoner. The thoughts bore deeper as I acknowledge the disappointment caused by my own stubbornness and selfishness that prevented my wife and myself from continuing our education. Awareness yanks on me like a restraining leash as I realize how bound I feel by my inability to be a better father for my children—I swore I wouldn't, but I'm treating my wife and children with the same roughness and neglect my father did with his.

I wince as my thoughts dig even more and insist on acknowledging my servitude to jealousy and weakness for sexual fantasies and libido-pumping film scenes. A cold sense of loss saddens me as I think of the years I've spent under the control of these agitations.

Still shuddering at this, a virtual image forms showing me trapped inside a tight cage-like circle of iron bars. I am above the image, looking down at myself. Each of the bars is labelled in the manner used in editorial cartoons—with the problems, attitudes, and behaviour traits I just mentioned. A quick glance at the labels confirms that these are not the only bars restraining me. There are others too—some I recognize, while others I inexplicably do not.

Hovering above this diorama, I experience an incredible sense of freedom. If the cell represents the state in which my mind lives it's no wonder I feel trapped!

Seeing this from outside ignites confidence within me and, like Tinker Bell pirouetting around the Disney castle, I zip about, doing loops and rolls in the sky to celebrate this break towards freedom.

Clang!

Suddenly I'm back. The image is gone and the flight is over, though the fresh and invigorating after-jangle of an exhilarating midway ride still races through me.

So, with my questions about slavery and freedom answered, how do I get free?

The answer to this appears to be in my hand. Though I realize it is not physically there, I sense that there is a key clutched in my palm, though I do not know how it got there. I understand immediately that it will unlock the door of my cell. My first reaction is to start for the door, but I abruptly stop midway.

What is outside that door? I only remember seeing the cell. If this is from God, is something expected from me in return for this escape?

I hate living in the confines of this mental prison, but I know the routine here and how to cope with it. Sometimes I even manage to find a small measure of comfort. Do I have to start all over if I leave? What if God really is out there and asks about some of the things I've done, and some of the things I've left undone?

My mental replay button clicks and one of those stories from Sunday school comes to mind. It's the story in which Adam went and found a hiding place after he disobeyed God. Is that what I'm doing? Why was Adam afraid, and why am I hesitant to leave this place and trust in God?

I look again at the key, sensing that it represents this person called Jesus. Somehow my acceptance of this man, and belief in what he teaches, will actually turn the tumblers of the lock, allowing the door on my personal darkness to swing open. This will set my heart and mind free of the consequences of believing in nothing more than the spontaneous evolution of the world. This key will work whenever I choose to use it. I am overwhelmed by this realization.

I sit in the cell crying, humbled yet lifted by the taste of hope I have sampled. I want to fly free, but I'm fearful; my logic does not understand how any of this can be possible. Finding enough trust to follow this process is surely going to change me, if I can do it. I have been looking for this a long time.

Gingerly, I slip the key into my pocket and sit down, not yet ready to use it. An unaccustomed peace accompanies my decision to stay and see what's next. The worries, fears, and doubts forming the bars of the cell still surround me, but for the first time I now feel that escape is an achievable probability rather than a hopeless dream.

Click.

I hear the sound of a lock releasing as I write in the notebook.

Welcome Mat
making the spiritual visible

ACTS 2:2

It's now my third day of doing this Bible reading and the day after that unreal experience of being inside that mixed up boarding house. The buzz I felt is calmer now but I am still in a whirl as to understanding what is going on. I thought about it all day at work and tonight I am anxious to see what is going to happen now.

The books take me to a single verse reading—Acts 2:2. It describes a noise from the sky that sounds like a strong wind. This noise then fills the house where the disciples and other believers were staying in the days following Jesus' crucifixion. I expect they were gathered with heavy hearts over the loss of their friend. The Bible records Christ having directed them to stay together in Jerusalem and wait for the gift of the Holy Spirit, whom he promised God would send. As they waited obediently for this unknown presence, wondering how it was possible for their miracle-performing friend to have his own life torn from him, I doubt they were expecting a wind to roar inexplicably through the hallways and rooms of the house in which they had sought refuge.

I laugh uncomfortably at their surprise. The clamorous activities of the boarding house again impose their presence upon me. I was not expecting God's Holy Spirit at all but, like those early believers, I certainly never expected a regal introduction to take place in such a disharmonious setting. Yet, indeed, that is what took place. How or why I cannot answer, but it happened.

There is nothing to see, hear, or touch, but someone or something else is definitely with me, not in an intrusive way but one that instils confidence and calm.

How did this Spirit get in the door, even though, using what I remember from the image, I had not undone all the locks? Entry was gained in spite of my reluctance to completely disarm the security measures. I recognize the contradiction in claiming that I want change so badly but continue to resist help when offered. Though I cannot explain it, I am somehow in conflict with my own logic yet I am feeling incredibly alive. I haven't felt this positive and hopeful for years.

My new found lightness is abruptly anchored by my sudden consciousness of the mess in the house—and just what or where is this house of turmoil and turbulence, anyway? In response, a new awareness stirs.

I am starting to recognize this soft yet distinct source of thought, or "voice," which is not my own and yet somehow expands my thinking beyond the limitations of logic and capability. I sense it will lead me to answers. It has to be God's presence in my life—there is no other explanation I can think of because so far, it keeps referring me to the Bible as a starting point.

As I sit here thinking, my clarity of thought and understanding is suddenly amplified—this Boarding House is a metaphor for ME!

This "visit" to the Boarding House is providing me with an opportunity to look inside my spiritual self. Even the most advanced medical technology can show me only bones and tissue—not what I'm thinking and feeling. The visual metaphor of the Boarding House lets me "see" the complex invisible structure of my psychological and spiritual existence.

All those locks on the door, for example, provide me with the graphic evidence to realize that there are many barriers within me resisting internal change, especially from this source called God. Last night, though, Jesus demonstrated that the only barrier he respects is my own will. I had to decide to unlock the door myself.

The noise, the disjointed activity, and the number of people amidst the clutter bring my inner turmoil to light. They represent a whole list of issues in my life which result in the shackles of distress, dysfunctional relationships, guilt, disorganization, fear, frustration, hurt, worry, rejection, anger, disobedience, jealousy, vulnerability and unexpressed love. They, and others—some good, some bad, are all squeezed together in my head. Now I can see them as the furnishings and tenants of my spirit—the Boarding House.

Though I live within its mincing effects every day, I have never before been able to see my inward unrest. I have always been subject to it and act outwards from it, giving it expression rather than management and maintenance.

If it is true that God created us, then the exquisite detail of the exterior image of the house witnesses to the thought, skill, purpose, and aesthetic integrity of its designer. Like me and my behaviour, the dilapidated condition indicates that it suffers from neglect, but by entering the house it is possible to see the extent of its disrepair and its cause—the chaotic life it contains.

Many times and in many ways I had set about to clean up my act, or, this house. My only accomplishment, however, seems to be to shuffle the tenants and clutter from one room to another. The security system at the entrance bears witness to my attempts to exist amongst the tenants as they move in and make known their selfish demands. I want to protect myself from any more barging in until some sense of order can be established. The locks provide some security, but now I realize they also interfered when Jesus called at my door. Perhaps he had tried before, but my preoccupation with the unruly tenants rendered me both weary and defensive. Even if I had believed in him, discerning Christ's knocks on the door from those of the thieves of hope would have been impossible. I had retreated to an anxious refuge behind the bolts and locks. No one was allowed in. I did not venture out.

Eventually, this house became a prison, growing ever lonelier in the midst of my bustle and confusion. Emptiness grew into a very heavy burden and a garbled cry escaped from somewhere within me. Christ heard that cry and came to the door once again, but I had to first unlatch the locks. This boarder came in only by invitation. There were no qualifying conditions that had to be bartered. I expect however, that I will be unable to trust and accept whatever God offers me through the Holy Spirit until I willingly give him access to all the rooms of my hideout.

That means risk. I do not want to feel vulnerable again, but I do want to change so badly. I want to trust this, so here I am, finally opening the door and allowing God entry to this bollixed boarding house called "me."

The noise, disarray, clutter, and clangourous relationships of the present tenants have me wishing I had cleaned the place up a bit before inviting in my new boarder. Actually, a full scale renovation would be more in order than a cleaning. I have only troubles, pain, confusion, and resistance to offer. Some welcome mat I have put out! How could anything useful be built from this flea market mess?

Is that what the Holy Spirit has come to do?

"In my Father's house, there are many mansions."

There are those words without a visible source again.

Full House

awareness of God's presence

It's night number four. I need some answers so I can figure out what's going on inside me. So far, each time I read some verses I discover something I didn't know and it feels good. Each session has also generated new questions and, new doubts. It is hard to believe that I now think God might exist and on top of that, I am reading a Bible.

I wanted to know something about the people being mentioned in the Bible before starting this time, so I found a web site and read a list that gave me a bit of background on many of them.

In this reading, Paul, the man who wrote this section called Corinthians to some church people in the city of Corinth, is explaining how God knows the contents of our hearts and minds, and likewise how we may know what our Creator wants for us. It is because of this Spirit again, who could live inside us. My head was already too full of thoughts and contradictions! What will happen now if I'm not the only one using the space?

I feel a twist of discomfort recalling each night's mental wrestling as I try to find sleep amidst my bad memories, my need to succeed in my work, my questions about the purpose of my life—if there is one, my fear and mistrust of my father and worries about my kids' future. They all combine with awareness of countless other failings and fears, eroding any possibility of inner calm.

My inner battles are kept secret though, because I don't want anyone else to know how uncertain I am or how scrambled my thoughts can be.

New Life in the Boarding House

These words, written to the Corinthians, indicate that someone else knows my private darkness in such intimate detail that nothing is left unexposed. I cringe from the thought as I think of reneging on that invitation to come in that I extended.

God's Spirit is identified here as the intruder. If I'm like a shabby old boarding house, then the "No Vacancy" sign must be up. Where is there any room for this Spirit?

I sit baffled for a time.

Is this how God works—from right within each of us?

I always pictured God as being remote and unapproachable, like a regal ruler scowling from a high throne. Edicts about our wrongdoing and pronouncements of laws to spoil our fun were the only utterances heard. A change in my perception of God is necessary if Paul's words are pointing me in the right direction. But like Doubting Thomas, I want proof.

I sense that this reading is pointing to the proof, my reluctant attitude being the only real obstacle to recognizing it.

Wanting to believe, yet still afraid, I risk contemplating a warm and caring God, envisioning what I think would comprise a perfect combination of mother, father and best friend rather than my current image. I could like the person this second image presents if it is possible. This thought makes me feel more drawn together, less fragmented.

I waver between being puzzled and being pleased that God would be interested enough in me to push through the barriers I put up and give me an opportunity to find something better. I thought God was supposed to be all about good people. I have a lot of bad stuff hidden in the unlit attic of my mind, does God really know about all that?

Paul, who is supposed to be one of the best examples of a changed life and one of the greatest teachers about Jesus, says it is also possible for me to understand God's thoughts in the same way that God understands mine. If this is true, a lot of change is possible, because I will be able to trust someone who knows me intimately and yet in spite of that is still able to love me.

Building Permit

cautious decision to continue

ROMANS 15:7–13, EPHESIANS 2:12–22

So, thoughts about this Spirit of God and of Jesus were on my mind most of the day. If, like they say, the plan was to send a messenger of hope and change into a noisy, political, violence prone world—why was Jesus without the acceptable credentials of ancestry, power, and wealth? I would think that you would want to make a big impression on all people regardless of their social, political, intellectual or cultural prejudices.

A handsome, well-spoken Herculean soldier in full battle regalia charging in on a magnificent war horse, brandishing a gleaming sword and followed by an equally impressive posse would probably have demanded everyone's attention and respect. He certainly would have appeared capable of accomplishing the task. In my opinion, a baby who grew to be a mild-mannered guy riding a donkey wasn't apt to inspire many followers, let alone commissions for sculptors to erect statues in parks. But that is what was sent.

How could this be a conqueror of evil?

Yet, today's first reading, from the book called Romans, says that our hope, joy, and peace will be dependent on our faith in him. Vague memories from vintage Sunday school stories about Jesus flutter in my mind. He paid attention to everyone he met, especially those who appeared to be the least able or acceptable in society. He freely shared with them, and anyone else who wanted all this love, knowledge, and power to which he had access. When challenged about his authority and credibility, his replies indicated the necessity of faith for understanding rather than intellectual capabilities. His fight against the physical and mental enemies of ourselves and our society utilized forgiveness and love, not troops and weapons. He was supposed to break down the walls that separate us from each other and God. These verses also mention the Spirit of God again.

Certainly, I would like to enjoy hope, joy, and peace, but I'm uncertain about this Spirit. Images from old horror films viewed during my teen years leave me with a questionable impression of spirits. This Spirit is somehow a part of God and Jesus and supposed to be found in anyone who, regardless of social, intellectual, cultural or physical status, becomes a part of every person who believes in and accepts the invitation of Jesus, the radical on a donkey. This Spirit supposedly dwells in you as if you are a residence of some kind and functions as a conduit between each individual and God.

Distinct discomfort rises within me. If God really has the ability to live within each of us, I could be in trouble. Does that mean my rejection of people who have hurt or angered me could be considered a rejection of God, if this Spirit is indeed in them, too? Does God's Spirit live in those people with gaunt faces who live overseas that I decided not to bother sending money for food and medicine? What about that person I gestured at in traffic the other day? Are those the kind of walls that Jesus came to break?

I'm getting a bit uncomfortable with my answers to these questions, so I decide to move on to the second suggested reading.

In the book of Ephesians, it describes Jesus breaking down a wall with his own body, a wall that separated people so that peace was brought to them and they were drawn together in union with him. This made them members of God's family who are to be built into a temple dedicated to the Lord.

This sounds a bit radical, and I don't really get it. These words about building temples trouble me. Certainly I am not interested in letting anyone build me into a temple, metaphorically or otherwise. The suggestion that I might be used as a brick in such a temple built to house God's Spirit is ridiculous. I am not the queasy, religious type who even goes to church, let alone who could be made into one. I don't want to be like them and even if I did, I've done some things for which I'd be rejected as substandard material.

How can anyone be a brick? What does the author mean by saying we will be built into a temple for God's Spirit? While spinning these thoughts around the thought occurs to me that if any of this is possible, I'm using my brick to build walls, not temples.

These thoughts remind me of the image of that grand yet neglected house—the roughness of its condition. If in fact I am like that, then a major renovation is going to be necessary before I can become any sort of temple.

Somewhere deep within me, a feeble yearning stirs. Oddly enough, the suggestion of becoming a brick in a whimsical building begins to fill me with hope—and it feels good!

If this Spirit can do this then I think I better get a building permit ready and see what happens.

Skipping Class
doubt

1 Thessalonians 5:16–22

My initial excitement sort of fizzled because of my resistance to the possibility of this whole thing so far and, along with a busy schedule, has kept me away from reading and prayer time for a few days. I promised myself I would stick with it, but it got added to my pile of other broken promises.

My mind has been filling again with worries and problems. My old logic leaks in as I ask myself how I can take precious time from such pressing realities to sit and talk with someone I cannot see. I'm feeling separated from what happened a few days ago—was it real or just a figment of my imagination?

It's startling how intense this feeling of separation has become in such a brief period of time. I have to stop my frenetic mental racing and try to reclaim calm thoughts. Though each matter before me threatens some dire consequence if left ignored, I finally scrape up enough courage to turn from the demanding cry of activity and head for the door—the door to the room where I go to be alone while reading the Bible.

At first, the sharp silence makes me acutely aware of my embarrassment. Sheepishly, I offer a halting apology for my absence. Though the space feels welcoming, I find myself being asked for an explanation for letting God's Spirit wait while I addressed the call of the hectic life I want changed. The question however, feels more intent on leading me to understanding than an accounting.

Several awkward moments later, I find myself suspended on the end of the pike pole of my logic. I feel its unsettling jabs. How can I ignore such pressing matters? What is that noise in the front of the car again? What should I do to help my sister with her problems? I can't find enough free time to finish fixing the front porch. Is this pain in my side something serious? How can I put more overtime in on that big project?

Listing these worries helps me realize how unproductive my response to them has been. I have worried, period. There has been no resolution. Nothing positive has resulted. At the time, however, these concerns seem to be overwhelmingly important. They dominate my thinking and actions. They crowd out my resolve to spend even a few moments of prayer time in the morning, yet this is the time that so far has provided unbroken promises of answers and comfort.

Why have I allowed myself to become bogged in the mire again? I don't want to feel this way, but as my unconvinced friends would chide, how can reading the Bible help me with these problems? What if it doesn't? God is only interested in church stuff, not my puny worries, right?

Before my questions are able to multiply further, today's reading is before me. The verses are short, but presumably because of the Spirit's presence, set off a line of thinking in me that warns me of ignoring what I have seen so far by holding on to doubt about God's desire or ability to be involved in every aspect of my life.

The negative power unleashed by doubt will quickly chop an opening in my thin faith, allowing me to slip back into the moray of confusion and anxiety. Once caught by these elements, my human logic will nag about the importance of these problems and taunt me into believing that solving my problems is up to me—no one else will do it.

These old patterns of unbelief can smother the opportunity for new life. God won't force me to read the Bible and talk to the Spirit—it has to be my own choice.

If I don't remember what these readings teach and try to make contact, I won't be able to hear God's voice. Then doubt will, like a shoplifter, quickly snatch the joy and thankfulness that has just been awakened in me and run off.

My understanding of what is happening is starting to change.

The virtual Boarding House is much more than an incredible experience or as old miser Ebenezer Scrooge muttered in Charles Dickens *Christmas Carol,* the result of "…a piece of undigested fat." Seeing the obvious dilapidated condition of it, and looking at the disturbing life that exists within it due to the clutter and conflict between its many boarders, enables me see why I feel so messed up and how I got into this condition.

What I am is not what God hoped for me—or any of us—to be. The Bible, which until recently I have ignored, appears to be like an operating manual, giving directions on how to build happy, constructive lives.

My familiarity with house renovation makes the metaphor of a boarding house the perfect way to show me what has to be done to change my life. Renovating can be a big job and I think I better start by understanding first what I was designed to be and then learning how to do it.

It strikes me the Spirit could use that big box building supply store slogan that states, "Do It Yourself — We can show you how". I expect these Bible readings and prayer times will be where I learn how to properly renovate my core spiritual home.

I better get back to class.

Restart Button
more questions, decision to resume search

ACTS 10:22–43

'm back again and determined to continue. The guidebook suggestion for today recounts a meeting between Simon Peter and a Roman soldier who, uncharacteristically for a man in his position, believed in God. The meeting apparently occurred immediately after each man separately experienced a vision from God. I now know what that can be like.

In his vision, Simon Peter was given a new understanding of God's intentions which flew in the face of society's rules of qualification and acceptance. The centurion had a vision that directed him to arrange this meeting with Simon Peter. Apparently even the disciples had to change their thinking on occasion, and obviously God sometimes used otherwise ordinary people to speak to them even.

Peter began his presentation to this centurion by saying he now realized that every person who believed in God—regardless of who they were in cultural, economic, or social terms—was welcomed by God. The disciple quickly reviewed the highlights of Jesus' work, John's baptisms, Christ's empowerment by the Holy Spirit, his death, and then his appearances after death. He told the Roman centurion about the charge Jesus left the disciples about teaching others what he had taught them. Peter ended his talk by saying that everyone who believed in Jesus could be forgiven for anything they had done wrong.

Quick, succinct, and to the point. Dry almost. Where is the exciting stuff I have come to expect following these readings?

I picture this centurion and his guests sitting in the cool shadows of a house during a hot mid-afternoon. They're listening to the story told by a man who knew Jesus as a friend and travelled with him, felt the embrace of the cheering crowds, and experienced the tension of facing those who opposed him. Peter also lived the terror of the events leading to his friend's death. Yet this account of his presentation seems to reduce this incredible story to dull, dry facts.

Near the end of this recounting, Peter refers to Jesus reappearing to only a select number of people three days after his execution. Why didn't he just march right out into the crowded market centres to display the result of God's incredible power over even our worst fear—death? My twenty-first century mind, accustomed to mass and social media coverage of every conceivable event, wants to bemoan this missed opportunity.

Think of the impact such a public appearance could have had. The news carriers of the day would have been clamouring to spread far and wide the news of how Jesus of Nazareth had laughed at the puny efforts of those who'd crucified him. It would have been a public relations coup. The news of his victory would have been on the lips of those at every board meeting and donut shop in the country with next-day courier efficiency. Instead, he appeared only to those who already knew and loved him.

A prod from within awakens a sense that my new boarder has a different view of this, so I rethink my conclusion, trying to be open to more than my own position.

It's not long before I have to admit that if he had done it my way, the most likely first reaction of people to a dramatic, well publicized reappearance would have been chaos and fear. After the initial shock, people would then probably change their thinking and decide to follow him, but their actions would have been motivated either out of fear or a desire for super power and immortality. Was that his purpose?

As I ponder immortality and self-image, it occurs to me that the words I've thus far seen or heard about Jesus indicate that anonymity, rather than fame, was his mantle. He spoke and lived in a way that eludes our marketplace logic of winning mass favour. No public relations consultant today would recommend such a focus in a campaign to attract new membership to an organization. Demographic studies indicate that such a leader would not find much favour, and few people wishing to maintain their credibility and social status amongst friends, neighbours, and family would consider being identified with such a leader.

Why then did this Jesus the Christ use what I consider such a poor publicity strategy? He had the power and intelligence to use only the most attractive approach.

Poked along I think by the presence of the Spirit and my experiences of the past few days, the shroud of incomprehension begins to lift as I pose the question, What did he come for? What he is offering is not for the people who are satisfied. Jesus is not offering material or social status. My expectation is that people looking for either of these would quickly drop out of the line once they discovered this.

He is not looking for the attention that politicians, professional athletes and entertainers constantly seek.

I think he is looking for people like me—people who are lost or hurting in some way—looking for something or someone that is sincere and trustworthy. I'm looking for someone to lift me up not put me down. Someone who can truthfully answer the questions in my head and heart. An extravagantly staged entrance replete with props, bands, polished entourage and media scrums, won't have much appeal to me.

These thoughts satisfy my question about Jesus' marketing strategy and let me return to the information in these verses. As I reread them, it quickly becomes clear that there is exciting and important content here after all. Peter is highlighting God's acceptance of everyone on an equal basis.

This addresses more than issues of gender, culture, economic, behavioural or social standing; it says that each of us, regardless what we have done or what we think of ourselves, have no need to feel unworthy or unacceptable to God.

The things I have done wrong in my life do not exempt me from God's offer and I must not let my culture-induced guilt and shame stop me. There are lots of standards, rules, and people around (including me) who will quickly point out why I don't qualify. Peter's lesson is that we are wrong when we choose to think that way—that such thinking separates us from God.

The flat, disappointed mood that followed my first reading of these verses is now replaced with anticipation. I'm seeking a genuine answer to a need that penetrates much deeper than a social or political advantage and this reading assignment says that is what Jesus came to deliver.

Plea Bargain
broken promises, lies and second chances

PSALM 51

T oday, the reading guide lists Psalm 51 so I commence my search through the Bible for this next reading assignment, fanning the pages back and forth, eventually finding it near the middle of the book.

This reading turns out to be a very eloquent plea from the rich and famous King David. History books and Christmas carols have previously introduced this powerful man to me. The story of this king sharing the bed of a lady who was not his wife, and later murdering her husband also peeps back from my memory. My initial assessment of the dullness of this book could be in error.

Royal King David was petitioning God for forgiveness, now that judgment was imminent. He was pleading for understanding and mercy, throwing in sundry promises of future behaviour should God look upon him favourably in the face of his transgressions. His conduct strikes me as being like a child who has been caught in the act of some misbehaviour and then tries to bargain and promise his way to a lesser punishment than is deserved—promises he probably won't keep. But what has this got to do with me, other than that I've done it myself with a number of people?

"What about unto me?"

Seemingly sourceless words are in my mind if not the room again. They jar my thoughts back to an incident that occurred during my early twenties. My family had all been summoned to my father's house because he had unexpectedly fallen seriously ill. In my impatience at waiting for the doctor's arrival, I went outside to exorcise my fear by kicking and swearing at various inanimate objects as they came into my path. In spite of the conflict and alienation I experienced from my father, the outburst ended with me on my knees voicing a tearful plea: "Let Dad live and restore his health, and I will do anything you ask of me. I'll even go to church every Sunday." Surely if deals worked for me in other circumstances, and if there was a God, a deal would work now.

Well, Dad lived, but guess who didn't show up in a pew on that or any other Sunday?

Yes, I understand all too well what David was doing and feeling in this story. He is recorded as having been a strong believer in God, accomplishing many great things because he sought to do the things that would follow God's will rather than his own. Here was a man who was supposed to have a personal relationship with God, had become experienced in matters of social and political responsibilities, and was in a prestigious position of authority over an entire nation. I start off laughing at his predicament because here is another big shot who got caught and now is squirming. Then it strikes me that I am just like him.

Moments like these are desperate ones. Observers might speculate about the sincerity of someone's passionate pleas, but that person is genuinely and acutely aware of his or her needs. In these times, clarity burns shortcomings and wrongdoings into an individual's consciousness. If caught, an immediate response is demanded. The pressure is on and there is an urgent need to get those ducks lined up in a row again to avoid punishment. The promises are real at the time of offering, yet those promises are not always kept. Why?

Mentally, I return to my perch on the branch with Zacchaeus. I want to think this out. My perspective of David's plight slips quickly from laughing at a buddy who has gotten caught in the act to empathy as I realize that the indictment in these words also includes me. Why haven't I kept my promise? How many other promises have I broken?

I don't remember. Yet now I see that, though I have forgotten them, they may not be gone. I am filled with a suspicion that those broken promises have gouged some holes in my personality, as a cut would to my skin, and those holes are being invaded the way bacteria infect an open wound.

I squirm on my perch. It's getting uncomfortable. Though my part in this has so far been to read and listen, my circumstances hint at the inevitability of an upcoming dialogue with the guy in the white shirt. I'm not sure I want such an encounter.

My thoughts suddenly shoot back again in time to witness a predicament I once found myself in after stealing candy from a store. I was only nine years old, but those moments are clearly etched in my memory. The goodies displayed by the older boys who had succeeded before me made it very enticing; they made it sound so easy. Resistance to the temptation eluded me, as did success.

In that shattering moment of confrontation with the storeowner, my back pockets stuffed with liquorice and jujubes, panic flooded over me as I desperately looked for a way out. The exit chosen was a quickly concocted lie—"I bought the ones in this pocket yesterday"—coupled with a deal—"But I was going to pay for the ones in this pocket on my way out."

Pete, the pudgy shopkeeper in a white apron who so often laughed and took the time to make conversation with us kids, appraised me for a very long time. This usually jovial man had often given me candies on previous visits and here I was stealing from him.

Finally, in silence, he accepted the extended quarter from my hand, seemingly oblivious to the pounding fear within my chest. It worked. Images of punishment vanished and I left, but I didn't return to that store until my adult years. Pete was long gone by then.

Unfortunately, instead of learning a lesson of honesty at that store, I learned it was possible to avoid or minimize punishment by bargaining, usually with a lie or two thrown in as well.

Courts today are full of such manoeuvres: pleas of guilt to lesser charges, offers of information in return for promises of clemency—anything to avoid the consequences of wrongdoing. This bargaining has always worked for me—until now. I have never given it much thought, though for some reason at this moment, I'm very conscious of my plea bargain when my father was sick.

Does Jesus know about that broken promise? Is he going to do something about it? Maybe it doesn't count because I wasn't convinced God even existed back then.

The account of King David has let me see my own story. I want to deny the possibility that this old Bible story relates so specifically and accurately to me. I want to say that it is just a silly old fable about a whining man who did the crime but couldn't do the time. But that's not what I'm feeling.

I feel hope again.

How can I feel hope at the same moment I'm feeling exposed for wrongdoing? How can I feel hope by reading these ancient words from a book I've ignored all these years and consider irrelevant? I sit in astonishment, recognizing and accepting something about myself while reading of this plea for forgiveness by a man history recognizes as being enormously wealthy, powerful, and popular. This was the kind of guy *Fortune* magazine profiles today.

David was known as a righteous man through whom God made his presence known in the world. He was a direct ancestor of Jesus Christ. According to almost any standard, a leader in this position of trust and privilege should not have violated it. David did not deserve to be let off the hook for his wrongdoing, but historical records indicate that his plea was answered and that he was, indeed, forgiven.

God chose to forgive and restore David to be a man of integrity, though David did nothing to earn it other than recognize and admit his wrong behaviour to God.

I wonder if the secret guilt I have stashed away has affected my ability to believe this whole church and God thing. I am afraid of a face-to-face encounter with Jesus because I am ashamed of some of the things I have done. I don't even want to use his name. Like David I need to admit all my junk to God, as an honest plea instead of looking for a trade-off.

If God accepted the confession of this man—despite his deeds of adultery, murder, and abuse of power—then maybe a new chance is possible for me as well.

"It is."

I hear words again.

The List
the naughty–not the nice list

John 4:5–15

It's now been almost two weeks since starting this daily routine in search of a new life. My intellectual capabilities have been teased, stretched, and strained by this experience. None of it makes sense measured by the standards society customarily uses, yet I have no question about the reality of the new activity in my mind. I'm actually starting to look forward to this quiet time each night.

During these times spent reading from the Bible, I've seen things through my heart that have both comforted and dumbfounded me. I have to say "through my heart," because it is like a virtual experience. The things I see in real life are the table and light beside me, the bookcase, some of the kids' toys on the floor, and the pictures on the walls of the room I'm sitting in. That I can even articulate being able to "see" with my heart is not something I ever could have predicted happening to me.

It would be easy to dismiss it all as I'm losing my mind rather than about to regain it, but for the first time in a very long while I sense it is the latter. I am no longer alone—not even when I am by myself. Since opening that door in the Boarding House, I have learned that everything I do and every thought I have is known by God, whose reality I no longer punctuate with a question mark. Likewise, my hunch about White Shirt's identity is confirmed by this activity. He is Jesus. While I don't have any concrete evidence to offer yet, I just know they both exist. There is no other way to explain what is happening. I also feel they want to give me something.

While confessing that my comprehension is absolutely minimal, I recognize that this Spirit of God is a vital link between God, Jesus, and myself. I'm still not sure who the Spirit is, but I sense there is a great deal more to be experienced in the company of the Holy Spirit if I agree to it. The hard wall of resistance I use to emotionally protect myself is shifting in response to the warmth I feel and welcome but do not understand. Somehow God, Jesus, and this Spirit are together in this. Like the woman in today's story—I am "thirsty". I want more of what I have had so far. I want my life to change.

As in the first encounter with the guy in the white shirt, getting me past my doubt has required a bit of shoving. At this point, however, I want to go on the journey. Much to my surprise, and contrary to my sarcastic belittling of others in the past who I have heard talk about taking such spiritual trips, I now realize that courage is require to set out on one.

Thoughts about David's appeal for renewal to God yesterday are still fresh in my mind. Images begin to flash through my mind of some of the things I have done wrong and the people I have hurt.

This causes me to flush with embarrassment. Using the battered boarding house metaphor again, if I was a house, there should have been a sign hung on me long ago declaring I was no longer fit for habitation—and instead designated for demolition.

Is this really what "temples" are built from?

As uncomfortable as the thought is, I decide to turn to a fresh page and start listing my sins. It isn't easy to do and yet I am shocked at how quickly the list grows down the page. Some of them seem so stupid or selfish, most of them I am ashamed to admit. Several of them brought tears to my eyes. I don't want anyone to see this list.

After finishing it, I reread it several times. I can physically feel the weight of all these things I have written. It suddenly occurs to me to do as David has done and read this list to Jesus, line by line, and tell him that I am sorry.

Apologizing is not something I have ever done well but I kneel beside the worn, plaid-covered chair, tears running down my cheeks, read the list in my hand and in a choking voice, say I'm sorry and ask him to forgive me.

I remained on my knees for a while before standing up but as I do, I feel lighter and somehow different.

Insurance Plan

everything has a plan

It's day thirteen, the list I wrote last night is folded and in my pocket. I can hardly believe what has been happening to me since that first night. There is even more going on in my thoughts than before as my mind keeps returning to these things I'm reading in the Bible, but everything else keeps banging on the door of my thoughts too—concerns like keeping my job, paying the rent, getting rid of the anger and fear that so often control me, the threatening thought I might be losing my mind.

Then along comes this writing from Matthew. Life sure seems easy for those birds it talks about! Have they got a MasterCard bill waiting to be paid? Do any of them burn with jealousy if his wife speaks to another guy? Are any of them afraid of their father and yet still aching for love from him?

It sounds like those birds have special protection. What protection do I have?

All around me are people, signs, and ads proclaiming what we already know: "Prepare for your retirement…NOW." "Invest for a better tomorrow." "Save for the day when the national pension fund runs dry." I get frightened when I realize that there is no cache of money waiting for me. I feel like a failure because I hardly provide for my family's present needs let alone the future.

There seem to be insurance schemes for every conceivable threat to your person or property. There are government plans to address every condition and ailment, including your rutabaga crop failure. There are long-term service plans to extend the life of your accumulated goodies, retirement plans that picture you and yours on a beach by age fifty-five, and investment plans that ridicule your desire to actually work for a living at all. There is a plan to save the whales and another to save our leaders in the event of terrorist attacks. You can buy a freezer complete with a food plan to keep it stocked, a dental plan to preserve your ivories, and a plan to stimulate the economy. In fact, for just about anything you can think of, there is a plan. Of course, there are always instalment plans if you can't afford any of the above today.

Everything is going by so fast. Zoom, huff, puff, and pant.

Watching all this activity and preoccupation over working towards tomorrow's provision and comfort draws to my mind the nursery rhyme, *The Three Little Pigs*. They worked their snouts to the bone until Mr. Wolf came along with his plan and rang the doorbell. Two of these pigs made a great barbeque. One of them however, did avoid the rotisserie roundup—because he had a plan.

I wish there was a plan for me.

These verses from Matthew appear to contradict our notion that there is nothing more sustaining us than human thinking and capabilities, that there is no other purpose and provision for us. We know that life has too few moments of triumph and can be frighteningly inadequate but can belief in the man called Jesus give us more?

It can't be that easy!

Common logic and prevalent opinion pressure me to understand myself as my own source. Yet here is this proclaimed shepherd of humanity, asking me to consider who cares for the relatively insignificant birds and flowers all around me. After doing this and accepting it must be true that it is God's plan to provide for them, he wants me to then compare how much more would naturally be given to people, who were the centrepiece of God's creation. The verses encourage me to find out more about God, realize I am not alone and without supernatural help and then *expect* I will be given whatever I need to live a changed life.

Though it sounds impossible and the people I know will laugh at this suggestion, I want to believe it. It sounds like a plan.

Doubt, though, slaps again at my flickering hope.

How can God look after all of us? Does he know how many people there are in the world? Can he really change things? Is there actually a plan for me?

What happens if I risk believing what I'm reading and it doesn't work?

"Fear not."

Light Switch

finding the plan, building trust

LUKE 9:57–62, 1 CORINTHIANS 2:10–12

So if there is a plan for me, this Holy Spirit and that image and understanding of the chaotic boarding house must be a part of it. The idea of the Spirit being here is kind of neat, though I'm certainly being more cautious about my thoughts lately.

There have been a few awkward moments, though. I never noticed before how easily I can slip into thinking that I would rather no one knew about, for example, those daytime fantasies about one of those so-called Baby Blue movies on late night TV or what I want to do to those drivers in traffic who insist on demonstrating their ignorance. I guess my point is that I haven't ever given much thought to controlling what I think about until learning that God knows every thought. Lately, I am putting a screeching halt to those thoughts. It feels even more embarrassing than the time my mother caught me flipping through the pages of a cheap picture magazine a buddy once loaned me.

Surprisingly, I am not finding this as intrusive as it sounds. There hasn't been any indication that there is a judgmental censor at work, randomly rummaging and poking around every thought in my head. Now that my self-editing processes have been engaged, it's actually becoming a bit quieter inside me. I like the absence of agitation.

There is also a noticeable difference in my thought patterns that feels very good. When worry or anger wells up, I experience comfort knowing I am no longer alone with it. A loosening of some sort has resulted from that awareness. In fact, my avoidance of indulging in fantasy (pleasant as it has always seemed) has lowered my emotional temperature.

Replacing my gray-bearded, heavy-handed ruler-of-the-universe picture of God with an inviting image of the caring father I have always yearned for has moved me forward considerably. My resistance yields as I discover these daily lessons bring me comfort. I'm looking forward to the one for today.

It's a short one, in which three men have a conversation with Jesus. Jesus asks them to follow him. The first man is told that the trip will involve some hardship and that there will be very few of the amenities he has come to expect from life. The second and third men each acknowledge their desire to go with Jesus, but mention an important family commitment that must be discharged first.

Instead of extending a congratulatory welcome, Jesus rebuffs them. The second man wants to fulfill his responsibility to care for his father until his imminent death before enlisting with Jesus' group. The third wants only to visit his family and loved ones to bid them goodbye.

To both of them, Jesus says, in effect, "That's not acceptable."

So much for the loving, accepting parental image! Disappointment fills me as the bubble pops. A cold shiver of fear skips across my shoulders. Am I supposed to desert my family, my home, and my job before God will allow me to move closer to Jesus Christ?

I can't! That's all I have to keep me together. How can God impose such strict rules on people who need love and understanding? Usually the people I've seen who live without homes and families don't look very happy. Are those street corner apostles who predict doom and gloom in God's name model followers of Jesus? Am I supposed to be like them and those door-to-door evangelists everyone laughs at and tries to avoid? I don't want to be like that. I thought we were supposed to look after our responsibilities. A dying father and loved ones at home are important. Do we have to give them up?

More questions, just when I thought I was getting better answers. Maybe I should give up. Even though I have found some really interesting stuff following this guidebook and Bible reading, I struggle with doing it. Dismay slinks around me until I think of this Spirit that is supposed to know God's thoughts as well as mine. If that is so, then maybe it has a better hold on what is going on here.

"Okay, Spirit, if you really are listening in, can you help me understand what these words are saying? What am I missing here?"

As soon as I ask the question, a warm feeling of having done something right washes over me. No voices or images appear though, so I decide to reread the verses. This time, those tart replies from Jesus seem to be questioning *my* reasons for not accepting Jesus' invitation to follow him and asking me to consider the source of those good things I don't want to give up.

The earlier explanation of how God provides for those birds and flowers—*and me*, comes back to mind. From that perspective, these verses now seem to be more about *trust*. Do I believe those words in the Bible that say God cares for me and will always and only provide what is good for me? Am I willing to trust what I am reading in the Bible?

If this is so, Christ's words aren't saying that I have to give up anything before Jesus will accept me. They are indicating that I need to decide which one I trust more—him or myself.

Looking back I realize that trusting in myself hasn't really worked so far. On the other hand, I have had some incredibly good results in a very short period of time simply from reading this paperback Bible, which is said to be the Word of God. To trust or not to trust—the right choice is getting clearer.

It looks like this read-along partner, the Spirit, really does have connections with people in high places, and a talent for mining meaning from a few words.

Each encounter with Bible verses helps me see and understand something more about myself. It's usually not comfortable to view myself from this outside angle but it is real and I'm feeling better because of it.

In certain past relationships, my trust or vulnerability was battered by people who knew about my weaknesses so I stopped trusting and sharing with others for fear of betrayal. Strange as it seems to me, I want to trust this presence of God in the form of the Holy Spirit.

I'm excited at the thought but is the Holy Spirit an it, a him, or a her—or just a wisp of something in the air? My anticipation assumes a slight tremor of hesitation as images float through my mind of ghosts and spirits as they've been portrayed in popular literature and movies—cutesy cartoons or the foreboding entities portrayed in science fiction movies. But if this Spirit is from God, it must be good.

Though I would rather God did not know about a lot of thoughts that cross my mind each day, I am convinced that this new tenant, has been sent to me from Jesus with nothing but love—and the objective of that love is to help me. I'm going with it, and my expectation is that I will eventually get control over those embarrassing thoughts.

The second reading—1 Corinthians 2:10–12—explains that God's Spirit knows not only our thoughts but every detail of God's thoughts and intentions and shares that knowledge with those who seek it through their faith in Jesus. Though I have often hidden my thoughts and feelings from other people, and even tried to stash memories and feelings away from myself, I now learn that there is no thought or need within me of which God is unaware.

My limited knowledge of physics and a quick guess at the population of my hometown—never mind the entire globe—makes it hard to understand how this can be possible. Yet everything I have seen and read so far says it's true. It also instils in me a sense of security and hope.

My understanding of the physical dynamics of this contact with God does not seem to be necessary to receive the life it brings. Belief and willingness are all I need.

"Seek and you will find."

Reading the stories in the paperback Bible is the method the Spirit of God is using to show me about God's reality and initiate the much-needed healing of old wounds to my psyche, setting me on a new path towards the future. With the Spirit's guidance, these printed words are able to unlock the doors to an abundant life—to a changed life.

Yet the same Spirit, filled with all the power and authority of creation, seemingly can be silenced by the simple act of rejection. I don't want to do that, I want the Spirit's quiet voice to continue using the lives of people in the Bible to explain my own life to me.

This third person of God, who is as unique in nature and purpose as the other two—God the Father and God the Son—is specifically and profoundly concerned with me. The Holy Spirit, whose presence and power were essential for Christ's work on earth, is now offering to be my friend, teacher, mediator, counsellor, and companion. Judging by the sample demonstrations I've seen so far, this unseen roomer could change my life. The master builder is willing to renovate my Boarding House into the temple it was created to be.

The "No Vacancy" sign by the front walk of the boarding house reappears in my mind. It reads the same, but my understanding of it now is that it signifies a new truth. It used to state the obvious condition of overcrowding. Its new meaning proclaims that the newest roomer is the only one needed or wanted.

I think the lights just came on.

Does everyone encounter God this dramatically? I know that a renovation of the Boarding House, my whole inner being and life, is badly needed—its beginning to look like not only is it possible but that it is going to happen.

"In my Father's house, there are many rooms."

Team Meeting
the purpose and participants in prayer

EPHESIANS 6:18–20, MATTHEW 6:6, EPHESIANS 5:15–21

When all this started, I was wanting to escape to a new life. Yesterday I discovered again that this Holy Spirit is in fact able to help me understand and learn from the Bible. I am feeling better now. It looks like the Spirit of God is here to help me personally, so I am going to carry on, though I am not sure to where.

The emphatic instructions in Ephesians 6 quickly indicate a serious lack of discipline on my part in staying in touch with God through prayer. They make it clear that I must invest some effort in prayer in order to hear the vital information the Spirit has for me. I also have an underlying sense that it may be necessary to present my needs to God more than once or twice before receiving an answer.

Ask for God's help. Do everything in prayer. Pray on any and all occasions. Stay alert so that you will hear God's will and let the Spirit lead you. Pray for God's teachers and people. Don't become lax or discouraged in seeking God's guidance.

I resist these thoughts at first. Surely, though, this does not mean God is so busy or hard of hearing that I need to repeat my prayers until they are finally heard! Or are these verses saying that my concerns are not important enough to bother God with? Are they saying that the Spirit will give me the appropriate prayers to ensure God will listen?

What is a prayer, really?

I remember bedtime prayers as a child that went, "God bless Mommy, God bless Daddy…" on down the line of family, including the dog and pet gerbils. I know the Lord's Prayer, which at one time was recited every morning at school during opening exercises. I am aware of one-line prayers cried out when danger or tragedy loom nearby. Why would you pray prayers like any of those throughout the day? How or why would God's Spirit lead in such prayers?

These questions led today's session towards a second reading, found in Matthew. In it, the reader is admonished to go into a small room or closet, close the door, and pray to God in private. According to this verse, God will meet you there.

Once again, I am utterly amazed. As I sit by myself in this room, in my beat up armchair, I find this verse describing exactly what I'm doing. These times are incredibly full of discovery, the discovery of contact with timelessness and hope and someone who loves me. This verse traverses time to answer my request for a definition of prayer.

Prayer, then, is relationship, because in times like this I know I am in the company of God in spiritual form, a form I now trust as a friend and constant companion. This friend obviously knows me in a manner that goes beyond even my own self-awareness. These times have been conversations through which I receive comfort and answers to my doubt-filled questions and requests.

My needs have somehow been anticipated and answered even when I have been unable to properly articulate them. Certainly my companion has led me to valuable answers for which I had not yet realized my need. Like the claims of deep heat ointments for aching muscles, these prayer times deliver love treatments that can penetrate an aching heart.

Thinking about my earlier prayer forms, I realize that they had no life because I did not give any life to them and didn't really expect to find any in them. The few times I tried could more accurately be labelled as request lists or woeful cries of self pity or sullen complaints. Even then, spewing them out quickly and then dashing off without waiting long enough to listen and see if God had something to say back to me. Yet these recent times reading the Bible have been abundant in the company and answers they've brought me. I know there's activity in them and their energy seems to be directly related to the love I am willing to receive and its reflective action.

My thoughts skip back to earlier lessons and the things I learned from them. One in particular taught that when two or three people are together and agree in what they ask God for, their request will be fulfilled. The discussion in which they engaged before presenting their request to God would filter out any selfish desires of the petitioners and develop the real need. If God's Spirit knows each person with the fullness with which he has demonstrated knowing me, as well as everything in God's mind, it is no wonder these writers advise us to listen for and follow that lead. Anything should be possible with such resources.

God is, through some mysterious method, able to be present in a tangible manner when we pray as the Bible teaches us to do. Just as we sit with a friend and talk about our problems or share our happiness, so too may we sit with God. He may not be visible, but he's real and present.

Private, troubling thoughts are usually stripped of their debilitating power by the exposure of being spoken aloud. The trusted person with whom you share these thoughts and troubles is able to offer company, encouragement, and a fresh perspective, which leads to solutions and new understanding. Conversely, happiness shared openly with a friend has the amazing effect of growing and splashing into the life of that friend, drawing them into your celebration. Conversations with God do likewise. There is no need for an agenda, just the intention of honest sharing.

The relationship of trust and confidentiality we enjoy with a friend is built over time through numerous conversations sharing our experiences from day to day. Good, bad, and in between, they become the fabric through which we know and depend on each other. We need a similar opportunity to build a relationship with God. These verses explain what I am coming to understand as I learn to pray with an open heart.

A wave of thankfulness washes over me as I absorb this new teaching and my understanding grows yet again. The importance of my Companion is reaffirmed near the end of the reading from Ephesians 6. Here the writer—Paul—indicates that only through the active role of the Spirit is it possible to fully understand the contents of the Bible. Prayer is the conscious act of meeting with the Holy Spirit and engaging in dialogue with God. Paul finishes by acknowledging prayer as the solitary link to his information and ability to teach. Prayer, to Paul, is a vital and integral part of life. Without it, he could not know God.

An exciting charge surges through my chest and vibrates in my arms and neck as I absorb this understanding about God's care and accessibility for me. Though realizing that others will experience it differently than me, I now know that I have been shown how God makes personal relationship with each of us possible. This relationship is formed and exercised in prayer. But prayer is more than a weekly, pious folding of hands or kneeling and closing eyes to recite memorized words or confessions. Relationship is formed in daily, full disclosure conversations with God, about anything and everything.

I guess what I have been doing for this past week or so could be called at least a form of prayer. I am reading from the Bible, asking questions and receiving answers—all with God's Spirit.

The third selection, from Ephesians, which I have dubbed the "Book of Plans," starts with warnings about the way you live and the company you keep. It makes a very clear declaration that unless you are trying to discern what God wants to give you in life, you are living foolishly and will be easily swallowed by the circumstances around you. My serenity is elbowed here as I remember the Mad Parade.

The difference is immediately clear to me. When I drift away from dedicating time to prayer, I am quickly absorbed again by the brusque turbulence of life and logic. Actually, "mulched" might be a more appropriate term. I don't need to contemplate Paul's words very long to understand their truth.

Paul goes on to encourage us to drink in the Holy Spirit rather than filling up on wine. This analogy causes me to compare those times of celebration when my alcohol consumption led to impaired thinking versus my moments of celebration with the Spirit, in which my thinking was clear and amplified.

Today's lesson reminds me to offer thanks to God for everything. I doubt this is a lesson in etiquette so much as a reminder to be conscious of habitually being so busy enjoying myself—or, conversely, moping in self-pity—that I fail to notice all that God provides for me. As these sessions lift the screen of unfocused and cluttered thinking, I begin to see that God has always been present. The combination of my own logic, stubbornness, bad choices and life's evolving circumstances has blocked my view of God.

It has taken a very long time for me to even vaguely begin to understand what I have done to myself. Until recently, I didn't think I had any reasons to be thankful, let alone a God to thank. But at this moment, I am almost overwhelmed by a desire to thank God.

I am so thankful that these timeless stories from God are true. I am so thankful that God is real and wants a relationship with me—in spite of everything I have done wrong and everything I should have done but failed to do.

I even embrace the last sentence of today's reading, which directs us to submit ourselves to each other because of Christ. Earlier, we were asked to submit to the Spirit's lead. My normal reaction to such a thought would be rejection, because giving in to others meant I was weak—bondage would result and others would look on me with disdain.

Surprisingly, my reaction now is not my customary one. Today I realize that my insistence on independent thinking and acting led to false pride and foolishness; my ignorance mistook them for strength and knowledge. Upon reflection, I see that the fruit this has born in my life is more like the meagre, scabby apples from a neglected roadside tree than the red treat presented to teachers.

Jesus' call for submission is actually an invitation to freedom.

The paradox that freedom can be had in submission does not escape me, but instead of producing rejection—it tickles my curiosity to understand it better. I want to learn more. Much more.

My comment a few days ago about my heart and mind needing a renovation comes back to me. If that is what the Spirit is here to do, then like any renovation project, the first thing on the job list is to have a meeting with the team, get organized and clear the work area. It looks like Pride is a tenant that has to find out there are going to be new house rules.

I feel good at the thought that this is what is happening to me.

Is just saying "Thank You" considered a prayer?

Crutch or Cape?
more doubt

I Chronicles 29:10–13

Yesterday left me hopeful at the thought these readings are the start of a plan to fix me. Doubt has returned though as I plunk down in this old chair, to spend some time in the "closet" as yesterday's reading in Matthew called it. Am I simply superstitious and foolishly falling for some old stories to give me enough strength to live? Is that overused put down about using God as a crutch actually true? These questions arise as a result of reading a magazine article that indicated Christians are being accorded less and less credibility in our society. These thoughts trouble me.

Intelligent, well-educated people in every walk of life dismiss, in various degrees and forms of articulation, the existence of absolute truth and a supreme and personal God. A pall of scepticism is cast over the emotional or intellectual qualities of anyone who holds such a belief, much less practices some form of worship. Denigrating labels abound in articles, letters to the editor, and television talk shows for people who voice their values based on their belief in God.

This causes me difficulty, because I certainly want acceptance and respect from the people who live around me. I cherish individuality and creativity as part of a rewarding life while ostracism and oddity hold little appeal. Every one of us wants to feel accepted and valued.

Being an openly professing Christian outside a Christian community but inside the boundaries of our politically correct, science-based consumer society can leave a person somewhat susceptible to being labelled as fringe material, an indictment that renders you less credible in society at large. I don't want to appear that way to others.

Presenting myself as possessing all those movie-hero qualities of strength, self-confidence, and fearlessness in spite of what I felt internally, certainly gave me a correct image according to the standards of the majority. Since the effects of my encounter with Jesus Christ, however, I've both seen and felt a distinct difference in the way a number of people react towards me.

Co-workers, neighbours, and family members are now noticing something different about me and demonstrate a wide spectrum of attitudes, ranging from puzzlement to outright rejection of my belief in God. In wider terms, I even feel separated from social norms by newspapers, magazine articles, and television programs. Excluding the Christian forms, all these outlets position belief in God anywhere between harmless foolishness and dangerous ignorance. This contrasts sharply with what I have been experiencing.

The incredible love and exciting awareness I've received during my slow acceptance of what I see in the prayer times causes me to flush with embarrassment at the flickering doubts that cross my mind. Why am I so reluctant to openly declare my relationship with God? Have I found something real and vital, or am I what those media types claim? Am I really just an emotional weakling grasping for an omnipotent god for support and a reason for being?

That cannot be true, because my experience has actually strengthened me. In my renewed strength, I am discovering that I still want to be in the life-breathing presence of God, even when his strength is no longer a perceived need. I am unable any longer to think of God and Jesus as abstract or theoretical figures. I live in a treasured relationship with them now. The only thing I've done to deserve this relationship has been to be, by my own appraisal, extremely undeserving.

I don't feel that I possess enough words in my own vocabulary to adequately express what I have witnessed and experienced, hence my use of analogies and metaphors. I am simultaneously confronted and perplexed by the realization that I now appear to be part of a minority of people who know that God not only exists but also pours out love and seeks relationships with those who take notice of him.

I want in one moment to be able to tell everyone about my encounter with Jesus—and about this new companion, guide, and friend called the Holy Spirit. In the next moment, I am too embarrassed to admit my belief in God when I encounter unbelievers. Previously I projected a perception that encouraged others to believe that I was a confident, self-sufficient individual with the prowess of the caped heroes in action movies and graphic novels. Have I lost that? Am I now going to be unable to walk on my own?

This discomfort accompanies me to the closet time and today's passage, from 1 Chronicles. Here I find a king whom history documents as being very powerful and successful, a ruler whose reign accomplished great advances in culture and social justice. This man's courage and intelligence earned him the respect of the vast armies he led to many victories.

My entry into this biographic profile of the great King David finds him addressing a large group of people, presumably distinguished members of his governing courts. In his words are found simple phrases that witness God being the source of all power and authority. David makes it very clear that he attributes all his talents and success to his relationship with God. He leaves no doubt about his belief in God and testifies to God's ability to transform any person.

David's dependence on God gives me insight into the definition of true strength. I feel honest admiration for this man based on affirmation, not envy. I'm filled with confidence and a desire to grow to have a faith such as King David professed.

As I put the Bible down, I feel pleasant calm in the realization that my definition of strength has been altered and raised—significantly. I am empowered by these stories of people who believe in God. I wonder if it isn't the holders and purveyors of disbelief who are the ones limping.

Another piece in the reno project.

The Toolbox
getting ready for change

MATTHEW 11:28–30, 2 TIMOTHY 3:16-17

My schedule lately has been so busy that the only way I made up a bit of time was to skip my morning prayer time for the last few days but I'm ready to get back to the project. Actually, I missed doing this. With the dawning of this new day, I'm determined to do my part to change those things about my life that cause me so much trouble.

On the commuter train to work, I jot down those things I want to be different about myself. After a few stops, the list comes close to filling a page. No wonder the rooms in the Boarding House have so much clutter in them. It is, of course, clear to me now that the clutter represents all the worries, concerns, and involvements I hold in my mind day after day. Some are responsible and acceptable while others are not, but there are too many for me to control and they constantly collide with each other, interfering with the normal, healthy functions of my life.

As I ponder the items easily lifted from the main rooms, or the ones closest to the surface of my consciousness, I revisualize the proliferation of stuff in the attic and basement. Those areas, which I seldom visit and which are not accessible to anyone else, hold even more items eligible for my wish list of changes. This is where the most bitter and unforgiving memories, habits, and attitudes are hiding. I am still reluctant to admit to or identify most of them.

My enthusiasm flutters for a moment in the face of the extent of the job before me. My toolbox isn't even open yet. None of these changes appear easy.

Some of the changes will require commitment and discipline. Other items on the list do not fit that description, and fit somewhere between being extremely difficult to impossible for me to change. Now graduated well past fluttering, my enthusiasm wanes even further.

I have felt this weight of frustration and futility before, on other occasions when I have attempted to acquire some control in my life. At those times, when well-intentioned advice and self-help books failed to satisfy me, I walked away, discouraged and conceding defeat. I tried to ignore those situations, unable to face the pressure and emotional strain. Like a shadow in bright light, however, those problems stuck close and chose inconvenient times to nag at me. A few times, my strategy feigned success for a short period of time. But eventually the true ineffectiveness of my solutions became obvious, allowing me to understand the dilemma faced by dieters and smokers whose resolutions produce long struggles and whose victories are too often snatched away in the end.

Just as walking through a long unused room excites dust into the air, these moments of reflection rouse within me the clutter of unresolved worries, relationships, and wrongdoing from times past. Failure and dejection pile onto my shoulders. A mixture of bitterness and self-pity moistens my eyes. I forget about the new promises brought by the Spirit for a while, as my thoughts bump along aimlessly through old, hurtful memories.

Eventually, an image of the toolbox I was so eager to open flickers weakly in my mind. A sharp, sarcastic laugh escapes my lips. What kind of tools can possibly make the repairs I need? Pneumatic drills and cranes won't be enough to get through all this. The metaphor was fine to this point, but now what?

I stare out the window at the passing buildings before checking the daily reading guide tucked inside my canvas sling-tote. Then I pop the tiny Gideons New Testament out of my jacket pocket and commence reading.

Jesus is speaking in today's reading, from the book of Matthew. He's talking about the loads we labour under. He makes a broad, all-encompassing statement which I am able to understand in the context of the struggle I am subjecting myself to in my desire to change how I think and act. Other people can perhaps read this narrative and see its meaning in the context of a physical need or a problem relationship. No doubt these words can touch many different situations where we feel weighted down with a problem bigger than we can handle by ourselves.

He makes a strange but straightforward offer. "Take my yoke," he offers. Take on his load and it will be one that can be carried without feeling tired or burdened. In a way, the statement doesn't make sense, but I realize it is telling me that there's no need to overwhelm myself with the responsibility of addressing every list item on my own.

Talk about timely messages! I read these verses a couple more times just to prolong the contact before returning to the list of behavioural and emotional clutter I want to dump.

I guess there are certain loads of responsibility, disappointment, loss, and guilt which each of us, because of our human experience, have to carry. Each of us is capable, because of our inclination and interpretation of circumstances, to add to that load, and we usually do. Many of us allow others to supplement our loads, and sometimes it seems as though life generally wants to pile extra junk onto our shoulders as well. This results in loads that are too heavy for us to carry. We protest, cry, and struggle, and sometimes if there is no relief we collapse under the weight of it. We often try to escape from our troubling reality through alcohol, drugs, or other physically abusive behaviours. This only adds destructive weight to the load.

Jesus' words in these short verses make clear that it is not necessary for us to carry such weight, and it certainly is neither his nor God's will that we do so.

Understanding the message in these verses, and placing our faith in him, will allow Jesus to teach us how to live without these crippling emotional loads which can be so destructive to our spirits. This is not to say that I can drop it all and live an unencumbered life without the weight of morality, compassion, or responsibility. In fact, I interpret the words spoken here as meaning that I will be challenged to carry a certain load that will be beneficial and necessary for my development. Jesus may even put items in my load that I normally wouldn't want to carry.

Regardless of the load that results, by going to Christ with each conflict, fear, worry, pain, and disability, it will be impossible to walk away with the unmanageable burdens I assume on my own. Jesus will show me how to carry, without strain and stress, those items I must and help me with those I cannot.

My attention returns to my list. Even if it was possible, it would not be necessary for me to do this work on my own. Today's verses make it clear that I have the option to take my load to Jesus, just as it is.

I finish by reading the second selection for the day.

Now, my toolbox is open.

Why Me?
feeling unworthy

Titus 3:4–8

continue to hone an acute awareness of the changes in my frame of mind. While retaining the residue from less sunny times and experiences, my thoughts voraciously absorb the observations and insights gained each day in my visits with God's Spirit. In these times, these verses continue to help me identify the problem areas in the Boarding House—the things that messed me up.

Though I can't explain it yet, I know my experience is real and, like the literary character Ebenezer Scrooge, I've finally become convinced that my attitude about life and other people needs serious adjustment.

Accepting the reality of these encounters catapults my thinking to a new dimension, promising incredible destinations. My vacillating eagerness and hesitation only exist because I am unable to fully grasp how or why this is happening to me.

God's Spirit is present and offering me a new life. My newly experienced sensations of pure love, coupled with the astounding insights laid before me and the resulting confidence of the discovery that there is a supreme God, have given me the desire to change and be changed. I now have enough courage to try for it.

Scrooge awoke from his adventure a transformed man, ready and anxious to amend his record. He finally understood why he should try to be a better person. Both the immediate time period and the future could be affected by whatever attitude he put into action each day. I am able to identify with his experience, albeit a fictional one, though thankfully mine contrasts sharply from the more macabre details. Like him, though, I need to change the basic operating principles and procedures of my life.

Hope is gushing into this Boarding House like urethane foam from an aerosol can, plugging the cracks and blocking the cold drafts of despair that previously blew through the house. Excitement, anticipation, and warmth scrub away grime with the determination of a car wash in the muddy season. The presence of God's love fuels me through each night's fitful dreams and each new day's encounters.

Again, like Scrooge the morning after, people who regularly come in contact with me have noticed changes, but my attempts to explain them always fall short, resulting in raised eyebrows. Their doubt-filled faces are the most difficult for me to handle. Their reactions often provoke an internal tug-of-war—believe it, don't believe it; believe it, don't believe it. "Believe it" has its anchor in my heart, while "don't believe it" is clearly rooted in my head.

The doubt that assails me most frequently is the question of my worthiness for contact with the God and Jesus of history. What on earth could have motivated them to not only notice me but also become so actively involved in helping me?

I have no enlightened response of my own to offer but I can see that there are numerous stories in the Bible about individuals whose lives were similarly touched by God. They too, were unprepared for such encounters and retreated initially, pointing to their own weaknesses and lack of worthiness. As their protestations were answered, their resistance yielded, resulting in new life.

But why have I been touched this way? The most significant deeds of my life have either been mean or selfish. I am only one miserable person among others who either have greater needs or display more obvious reasons for deserving God's attention. So why choose me?

I find answers on this day of doubt, in four short verses in the book entitled Titus.

Once again, a specific need is met at the exact time I think about it—not before, nor long after, but precisely at the correct moment. It's like the verses were written just for me. This has happened several times since the arrival of the Holy Spirit! The timely response leads me to reflect about this unseen person in my life. It is a welcome presence, not intrusive as it sounds. It's very gentle, easily unnoticed at times, and yet powerfully and decisively present.

Thinking back to that first meeting with Jesus allows me to see how my understanding and beliefs are growing proportionately to the development of my relationship with the Spirit. There is even a new ingredient in my character mix—trust. I stopped trusting anything a long time ago.

By allowing the Spirit to enter my life, it has become easy to recognize and see God more clearly in everything around me. As I invite the Spirit closer, my emotional and spiritual being somehow gains its intended lustre and shape. The relationship is becoming a friendship and through the universal dynamics of friendship, even though this friendship isn't about playing baseball on Mondays, swapping jokes, or meeting for lunch, my consciousness of God is opening. Certainly I no longer question God's existence.

Here, in the twenty-first century where the knowledge and logic of science are held in the highest esteem, I have been introduced to the power that science is trying to explain. Out of the deep, grey pit of my own stubborn denial and self-dependence, I have been hoisted into the sunlight of friendship with my creator.

I am starting to see that the stories about God we have all heard, the ones I have either dismissed or carelessly ignored, are true. Not only are they true, but they fall far short of expressing the whole truth. This being, God—who famous theologians, artists and writers throughout history have vainly tried in sundry ways to capture and quantify—in some logic-defying way, has entered into my life. God has chosen to be seen and known by me. God, who brought together the elements of matter and formed nature and us, who has been known by people across the millennia of history, who knows each and every person in creation and awaits each of us at life's end, has called on me.

Though I thought it would, the kind of person I have been obviously doesn't disqualify me from this opportunity.

A flash of doubt chills me. Everything sounds so great, but I've messed up so often—how can it be possible? I want to start afresh, but dare I hope it is possible? My eyes turn back to the words in Titus and their message, which says that it not only can happen, but that it *will* happen.

Crown Witness

looking for models

DANIEL 3

My high from yesterday remains with me as I start this day. This assignment is found in the Old Testament part of the Bible which is the time period before Jesus' birth. In Daniel 3, a powerful ruler declares a law requiring all the administrators of his domain to worship a huge statue of gold he commissioned to be built. He obviously understood the power this would exert over the subjects of his political conquests.

At the appointed time and place—amidst music, pomp, and pageantry—everyone came forward and obeyed the king's will. Most of them probably gave it little thought and simply did as they were told. Gullible ones may well have done it convinced that this was a bona fide god, while those whose hearts held only emptiness showed up hoping perhaps this latest god was the answer to their needs. No doubt others disagreed with the edict, or else had no opinion either way about its validity, but for political reasons decided it was most expedient to obey.

In some ways this society is not unlike our own. As a whole, we slip to and fro as evolving academic thought, laws, and social trends demand their acceptance and then are eclipsed by the next new supposed truth. We continually suffer the consequences inherent in this kind of society, which is so vulnerable to whim and weakness. Our rejection of the concept of being in a created universe ensures the continuation of instability.

Few of us challenge the status quo. Fewer still are able to believe there is a God and strive to live their lives accordingly. I wonder why. The quick answer given by many is, "God does not exist." I must admit that it's difficult to find and believe in the existence of something you cannot see or touch. Yet many people have been able to do it. The trouble is that these people are hard to find and for the most part the rest of us doubt their claims. We often seem to be without understanding of why we are doing what we are doing or where we are going. Many claim to know the right way, but everywhere you turn is littered with unfulfilled and broken promises.

This situation applies well to my own life and how I respond to the movement and values of society around me. Only since meeting Jesus have I had something to focus on that doesn't evaporate. Until now, nothing has remained at the centre of my attention for any length of time. As each new thing came along, I rode with it, hoping to find whatever was missing in my life.

I watched other people to see what they valued. Sometimes I would try what they had: houses, careers, hobbies, sports, physical prowess, family, etc. The list was long, but far from satisfying. This troubled me tremendously, until in my desperate examination of these other people it became apparent that many of them were just as unfulfilled as I was. If their emptiness was not expressed verbally, it was usually evident in their actions.

The ones who appeared on the surface to be the most complete were often revealed by examination to be focused only on self-fulfillment or morally question-able activities. Though disturbed, I associated with these icons of illusion for brief interludes. Fortunately these associations failed, not through my realization of their emptiness as much as my awareness of their potential to dominate me. I had little control in my life and turning over the wee portion I had was not an option.

Now and then, individual people who proved to be different would come to my attention through television programs, magazines, books, or the occasional personal introduction. They variously excelled in many forms of human endeavour, and each helped me by their example. I studied them and tried to follow their paths where I could.

Two of those people affected me more than any others. One was an internationally successful man whose autobiography I had read; the other was a local person known by few others apart from co-workers and members of a youth organization I was involved with.

The first, who possessed all the recognizable attributes of strength and authority, academic standing, business success, respect, attractiveness, and social standing, made a public statement about something he valued beyond his status. He said that the most important aspect of life was his relationship with God and living that relationship daily, in prayer and action.

By the standards of our techno-science society, this amounted to an admission of foolish weakness. In my need, however, I saw it as a sign of strength.

His autobiography gave me clarity and lifted my sights above my own small, troubling world. His writing expressed his own feelings upon encountering challenging situations in life. He told of his mistakes and shared stories of where and how God had entered in, enabling him to persevere and overcome obstacles. He freely declared that God's presence went far beyond survival and gave him an enthusiasm and purpose for life. His obvious vitality aroused my curiosity about God and ignited my desire to want a new direction for my life.

The second person to capture my attention was gentle, quiet, and very effective in an organization my son had joined. As I observed the operations of this organization, I was impressed by the way problems were either avoided or resolved by this man's genuine care and concern for people. His always calm and happy disposition distinguished him from everyone else. He was different, in a real and positive way. All those who worked with him were able to grow in their own confidence and competence. His hallmark traits were wisdom, inclusiveness, and dedication.

His unselfish submission to service had a profound impact on me. In time, I discovered that this man, too, freely admitted his faith in God. Though he was well-educated and had an impressive career, he did not take advantage of the status such achievements should have accorded him. Instead, he always displayed honest humility and transparently acknowledged his faith in God.

The notion of believing in God met resistance in me at the time, but I suspect a seed was planted as I decided to imitate what I saw and received from these two men.

Something in my reading of Daniel 3 prompts my memory of them. What is it?

It would have been easy for the three men in this story—Shadrach, Meshach, and Abednego—to acquiesce and go along with the crowd. What difference would it make if they simply pretended to worship the king's statue? They and their families knew what beliefs they truly held. Why risk trouble to prove it? By anyone's standards, they had a lot to lose by refusing to obey—their high-level government jobs, financial stability, social and political acceptance, and the well-being of their families. They risked it all. I think they are foolish. I would have been only too happy to have all that they did.

The new boarder nudges me, indicating that I may have missed something. Further reflection seems appropriate and it isn't long before I'm able to appreciate that I, too, enjoy many of those same benefits of social abundance. Nevertheless, happiness and satisfaction eluded me.

What was so different in their lives for them to find disobeying the king worth the risk? This question causes me to discard my surface quips and examine my resistance to the story at a greater depth. My initial judgement dissolves as I soon discover a healthy admiration for these three people. I admit I would like to have their level of faith and strength. They would not deny their relationship with God. They believed God could save them from peril, but made it clear that they would not change their stand, even if they were not rescued.

That is conviction. Their faith stirs me deeply and prods me again to find the same for my own life. It occurs to me that if their example is able to move me so much by merely reading about it centuries later, how much more meaningful would it have been for the people of their day, those who witnessed their determined stand? It seems reasonable to assume that their display of faith influenced many others whose stories were not told. Even the king, whose authority and stature was challenged, publicly acknowledged the impact their faith had on him.

There must be many others like me, who want to find and believe in God but need help in building a bridge to cross the credibility gap. It seems difficult to do. Watching someone else in his or her response can be very encouraging—necessary, even—to take the risk of crossing over.

If those three men had not insisted on worshipping God in an open, honest manner, without compromise to suit circumstantial standards or personal gain, they never would have been noticed. Those who were watching them would have been let down, and perhaps robbed of the courage they needed. The stand these three took became an example for all who witnessed it—including me.

Until now, my focus has been on the immediate benefits available to me through God, Jesus, and the Holy Spirit. This reading has nourished my own needs once again, but it has also shown me how God works with us through each other. Our experience of God is intended to be lived out by ourselves and seen by those around us. I am helped by watching the honest and humble witness of others who model genuine greatness. Will I ever be able to grow enough to one day be a helpful example to others?

Perspective
seeing the unseen, finding the emergency exit

2 Corinthians 6:14–18

My first reaction is to disagree with the message of today's reading. The writer is Paul again, this time with a letter to church members in the city of Corinth. The directness of the letter implies that they've already had such letters or discussions before. He is warning them about the impossibility of working with people who do not believe in God and admonishes them to separate themselves from such people. That seems foolish to me. I will be a lonely person if I follow this instruction and, besides, it hardly sounds like an attitude of love.

All the stories I've ever read or heard about Jesus place him amongst every manner and condition of people, and rarely with anyone who has acknowledged believing in God until after their encounter with him. The people Paul is addressing are not going to be able to help other men and women learn anything about God if they remain an exclusive little group that talks only to each other.

If a church follows this it would result in strangers remaining strangers.

I don't understand why Paul would teach this. I suppose such a policy does protect church groups from the secular influence of society, but what happens to the outsiders who, out of ignorance of God and lack of hope, never find a way in? Jesus didn't ignore them.

As I contemplate this paradox, I think too of how, at times like this, the Spirit comes alongside me like a tutor. This enables me to explore the concepts and words being introduced to me, words that sometimes baffle my intellect. So far though, this company always leads to a better understanding.

The Spirit doesn't just boost my intelligence like an optional plug-in smart board for the human computer. Instead, the Spirit gets me thinking from the "heart" that I am beginning to think is within every created human being, regardless of temperament style or personality type. Most of us, for one reason or another, either haven't exercised it or have chosen to ignore this component of our intricate bioengineering. My time in the "closet" as Matthew refers to praying, gets me in tune with this eternal part of myself in joyful, awkward, hopeful, unsettling, and invigorating ways.

I offer a brief prayer of invitation to my boarder, the Spirit, and almost immediately find myself and Zacchaeus sitting together on the virtual tree limb again. This easy-to-visualize metaphor offers an excellent vantage point! Some people may not feel safe sitting on a tree limb, even as a metaphor, preferring instead to use a grassy hillside or a risk-free monitor screen and ergonomic office chair. The limb suits me perfectly. It seems the Spirit is able to bring each of us to an individual setting that works best for us. This perfection of detail is a sure indicator of the Spirit's work.

Right now, looking out from the limb's elevated perspective, I'm beginning to think that there may be a fuller, more positive meaning contained in Paul's words than the literal interpretation I have given them.

One of the things I have learned so far is that it is clear the Bible is always including and addressing whoever is reading it. God never excludes anyone from receiving the message and opportunity of becoming a member of God's family. Keeping the Bible in small circles of people for their exclusive use waiting for seekers of truth to come to them doesn't make sense. Zacchaeus' story, and even my own at this point, demonstrates that God comes to us.

Certainly people exclude themselves after rejecting God, but those exclusions are self-imposed and never come from God. Based on this knowledge, it's safe to assume that Paul is not teaching these church people to do otherwise. Therefore, my first interpretation must be incomplete.

What is Paul doing then? His words are strong and obviously not meant to be ignored.

As in previous lessons, the Spirit prods my thinking to look deeper. Perhaps Paul's words portray the danger implicit in not fully understanding how different the values and objectives of the secular world are to those of God. It is a warning about compromising what God has taught with the seemingly innocent inclinations of our own logic. God's hope is for us to be certain enough in our knowledge and faith to be able to go into whatever small corner of the world we live in and bring to it an awareness of God. We are both spiritual and physical beings and Paul warns us that the world will change us if our knowledge and direction are not built on God's Word. The unseen but real effects of our ignorance about God, and the resulting acceptance of ungodly ways, can harm our spiritual lives. I think of the rivers and lakes around us. They appear serene and beautiful, especially under a sunset, and yet we know that hidden but lethal pollutants are endangering many of them.

Many sectors of society today are armed with reasonable logic that will sweep us along with the worldly tide. Science, for example, has become so credible and exhaustive in its offerings that it is hard to refute evidence suggesting humans are nothing more than highly evolved animals, capable of creating and controlling all that they survey. Rather than seeing science as the discovery of how God created the world, we are tempted to interpret science as a denial of God's existence.

We are led to view organized, structured bodies of business and government as being the sources of our security and physical needs. Very few of us are able to put more trust in God's provision than in a cheque from the government. When faced with a headache at the end of a trying week, it seems easier to swallow a couple of pills than spend twenty minutes in prayer with God, confessing our hurts.

We adopt these ways of living and thinking because friends, family members, and people we admire have also adopted them. There is, of course, some truth in these paths, but we need to recognize their incompleteness. Our own logic and the abundance of temporal rewards offered by these secular beliefs make it difficult, if not impossible, for us to resist them. Compared to the tangible visibility of the secular, the sacred appears to be quite inefficient, if not futile.

Aided by the change in perspective and clarity of thought the Spirit gives me, I can see Paul's words in 2 Corinthians are not telling us to remove ourselves physically from this secular world. He is attempting to draw back the curtains of human habit and reason to reveal a truth beyond our wonderful but limited capacity to understand who we are and why we are here.

Paul addresses the need for vigilance to protect our faith in God from erosion by the elements of any system that does not recognize and honour God. We have to live and work surrounded by secular elements, but Paul reminds us that instead of being swept away by them, faith in God will keep us from being caught in the undercurrent of human pride. Developing faith in God happens through prayer, reading God's Word, and with the guidance of the Holy Spirit.

Like a boat ride, life can be quite exhilarating until you hit turbulent white water. When you do, it's wise to have had proper training and a flotation device or a low-hanging limb handy.

As I'm rushing along on the current of daily life, I want to know there's always a low-hanging limb—like this one with the Spirit—for me to reach out and be lifted onto. I can see things better from here.

The Plans
figuring out what the Bible is

2 TIMOTHY 3:15–17

Thus far, in reading the Bible and learning to pray a bit, I have experienced some incredible moments and changes within me. It looks to me then, that with Jesus the carpenter as project manager and the Holy Spirit as the site manager, the Bible is the blueprint or plans for this renovation of my heart and mind—the Boarding House.

I want to know more about the plans. Can I believe everything written in the Bible? It *is* very old.

I started by looking on the web where I found a lot of garbage from confused or hurting people. Also found some good stuff. A quick phone call to the pastor who first helped me, produced some excellent, well-informed sources and books to check out.

Before long, I learned about the many versions of the Bible available today. Each version has been translated from an earlier version, often from a different language. Many people have been involved in this process, not only in contemporary times but also throughout several thousand years of history. Given the constant evolution of political correctness through the centuries, I wonder how the message and details in this book can be accurate if each writer, in a different time period, worked under the influence of his or her culture's prevailing social and political standards.

This question lead me to resource books that yielded details about this book everyone has heard about yet so few seem to understand. Within them, I found a few surprises.

First of all, modern scholars admit they are not able to be absolutely certain about the identity of all the original writers of the books of the Bible. They do know it was certainly not written intentionally as one book. The sixty-six books that make up the Bible are placed in a logical order, but they are not chronological. The book of Mark, though third in order in the New Testament, was actually written as many as twenty years before the books Mathew, Luke, and John. Together, those four books are known as the Gospels, a word from the old Anglo-Saxon word *godspel*, which meant "good tidings"—or in contemporary English, "good news." Also, the book titles do not necessarily indicate the author's name. Matthew, Mark, Luke, and John were not all members of the original twelve disciples, as I assumed. Paul, the great missionary who is credited with writing many of the books in the New Testament, was actually the earliest New Testament writer. He wrote them as letters to the churches he founded, intending them to be used for teaching, correction, and guidance. They date from approximately twenty years after the crucifixion of Jesus. Most of this I didn't know, and the little bit I thought I knew wasn't completely right.

There's more, but this small dose of knowledge is sufficient to raise even more questions about the authenticity and accuracy of the Bible. It defies logic to assume that its contents are valid after its incredible passage through time and human frailties. Yet I desperately want a new life and this "temple" Paul writes about sounds promising. What is this book called the Bible?

With this question in mind I come to the short reading for today, written by Paul to his apprentice, Timothy. Here, I find precious affirmation to counter my nagging doubts. Clarity and illumination break through the intellectual fog and my question is answered. This passage from the second letter of Timothy explains to my heart that which seems unexplainable.

Combining these verses with what I learned from my research lets me understand that the books of the Bible work because that is God's purpose and intention for them. The Bible then is a like a letter from God to us. God chose and inspired each and every individual throughout the centuries who worked to create, understand, preserve, or distribute this manual of love and life. Through the interactive work between God and the people chosen for this responsibility, the Holy Spirit has ensured that the basic truth in the Bible remains constant, though multiple languages have been employed to carry that truth throughout history.

Reading the Bible with the guidance of the Holy Spirit, as I have been doing, ensures that absolute truth will be revealed to the people who seek it. Without the involvement of its custodian, the Bible can be viewed as nothing more than a good book about morality, ethics, and antiquated laws interspersed with interesting case studies. The literal statements of these Scriptures are not the units of measurement for their own credibility, even though many people try to use them that way. The Scriptures are merely the vehicles through which the Holy Spirit brings true understanding to the genuine seeker, and with that understanding comes personal renewal and relationship.

These words then, are not to be reinterpreted to fit my own limited understanding. Nor should I twist and wring them to get their support for some new matter of convenience or argument. The Scriptures are to stand as they have been delivered to us. Many languages and versions, suitable for every individual preference or need, are available for our use. God inspired writers and translators, each in his or her own time period, so that the message would be available through the ages to every person born.

Men and women have received it, believed in it, and been guided by God to perform the many duties necessary for others to have the same opportunity. This amazing process has crossed history and every conceivable obstacle. In every era, men and women have one by one had their lives transformed and linked with those who preceded or followed them.

Starting from spoken words and written in only three local languages, the message of life has been translated into all but the least known languages in the world. Every medium, from clay tablets and wall paintings to modern-day printing presses and digital distribution, has been utilized to preserve and distribute God's message to us. I think of all the individual people God has touched and guided through the Holy Spirit to accomplish this task. It is an incredible testament of God's care and love for us.

There is more meaning and purpose for the Bible than simply helping us feel better or using it like a board game to collect rewards for good behaviour.

The Bible then, is like a letter from God to each and every person who reads it, telling the story of God's people as they face the problems of life in this world and celebrate God's place and victory in those trials. It explains why I may have hope and expect the promise contained in that hope. The example of Jesus is a goal and benchmark for me to use in my own life. The Bible contains the plans by which human temples will be built. It tells me that Jesus came and went through trials so that I could have another chance.

As I come to the end of this session, I feel much more confident in the benefit of reading the Bible. My trust level is rising. I don't think I can afford to limit my acceptance of the Bible to my own assessment of it by logic anymore.

The Apprentice
more trust, decision to honestly try

ISAIAH 55

My acceptance and confidence in the ability of the Bible to bring change to my life has bounced up and down so far. My heart wants to grab on and go for it while my head still wants to say it is impossible.

Yesterday's reading raised me significantly and greatly reduced the volume of my head's protestations. Today's reading assignment looks like it will settle the question once and for all for me.

This chapter of the Old Testament book by the prophet Isaiah grabs me in a bear hug. It starts as an invitation to a better, freer, more abundant life and ends with the promise that it can be delivered.

In my research effort a few days ago, I read that the Bible is also referred to as the Word of God. Verse 11 here vividly brings that to life for me and gives me a strong sense of conviction that yanks away the remaining doubt hanging over my mind about what the Bible contains. God's intention and ability to deliver are stated so powerfully and authoritatively that I see it as a promise of what I will find—a promise that will not be broken.

Thus far I have been popping in and out of the Bible in random order according to the list of readings for each day. It has amazed me what I have found there and how those discoveries are affecting me. There is so much I have learned already and I can see there is more to come if I accept the valuable apprenticeship this renovation project is offering me.

The opinion I had of the Bible is wrong. Proven by what I have experienced and learned during the past three weeks. I suspect there is even more for me yet in this book I thought suitable only for the fiction department of a museum.

I now see it as a very relevant time traveller, helping me see my past, fix and deal with the present, and build a changed future.

I think the new life I want is contained in this book—the Bible, and my relationship with the new boarder—God's Spirit. There is much for me to learn from them.

Building Consultant
reference source for building a life

1 Corinthians 3:1–18

These direct, no nonsense verses from the book of Corinthians were written by Paul—probably the most traveled, and certainly most published, early Christian teacher. This letter was directed to the people he previously spoke to in the church in Corinth but I see two valuable lessons here for everyone.

The first is this: it's vitally important for people to learn about Jesus and God. Paul knows this information will change their lives if they listen and follow it. He is aware of the void men and women will live and die in if they don't know about this message from God. His genuine concern for all people is obvious.

Genuine concern for strangers is a unique human characteristic. From what I have seen, Paul demonstrates that he is concerned for people wherever he goes. He expresses it strongly and must surely have been received by many people with dubious reservation, or even outright disbelief. My somewhat suspicious nature prevents me from immediately trusting anyone who introduces himself or herself by professing to care about my life and problems. Why would anyone do that for another person—a stranger even?

Paul did just that though, as did Jesus and the prophets who came before him and his disciples since. There is something special about a person who can love you not because of who you are (maybe even in spite of who you are), but just because you are. People who recognize and treat us as children of God, even though we ourselves may not know it, are living God's will.

The second lesson seems to be the importance of constantly evaluating how we are living. Paul is critical of the Corinthians behaviour in spite of the teaching they have received. He is concerned for their well-being and wants them to benefit fully by getting it right. He emphatically makes the point that they are still living by the habits and standards of secular society. Paul tells them that using such a model for their relationships with each other, and in building the church, will not work.

He reviews his earlier teaching to them and, using the metaphor of a building again, Paul describes how individuals construct their own lives, each according to his or her own resources and will. Some people have a wealth of resources to work with, while others have very little in the way of material goods or opportunities. Some individuals have to work hard and others appear to have it easy. These distinctions, however, do not determine the quality of the results. His words make the point that it is the foundation upon which a building is constructed, and the quality of the workmanship, that will determine the long-term value of the finished building—or life—when assessed by Jesus.

Paul says that Jesus and his teachings are the only foundation guaranteed to stand the test of time. Starting with that base will allow us the freedom to construct a unique life. He infers that Christ's intention is not to restrict us, but to protect us. Any life built on a foundation other than Christ will eventually fail.

Today's verses stir discomfort in me. I'm resistant to the announcement that there is only one valid foundation. My independent, creative nature wants the freedom to build whatever I choose. I want to decide for myself what I am going to build!

Come to think of it, I guess I have been exercising that freedom for many years now. No one has interfered, and what I have is exactly what I've built. The problem now facing me is that I already dislike the results. It has not worked out the way I planned. Until bumping into Jesus, I didn't think I had any other choice but to live in the trap I built for myself. My new tenant, however, is offering to help me renovate this place, and to be up to code and stand the test of time, we need to start with a solid foundation.

Paul reminds us about the importance of being a home for the Holy Spirit. As project manager the Spirit obviously cannot live comfortably in an improperly constructed building. Paul tells the Corinthian church that this analogy applies to us as we build our lives. If we ignore the sound engineering principles God offers us, the rest of the structure will not have the strength and integrity to withstand time and use. It will not be able to fulfil its purpose and ultimately will come apart one day.

This reminds me of a short film I once watched of a large building buckle and fragment, in slow motion, collapsing into a pile of rubble and dust. There have been a lot of days when I felt like that building.

My life—as seen in the Boarding House—is the proof of the truth in Paul's words. It is also proof of God's concern for me. In spite of, or maybe because of, the ramshackle condition of my "building," the Spirit accepted my invitation to move in and assist in the renovation project. His arrival ensures that everything necessary can now be done according to God's specifications. A leaky roof, draughty windows, squeaky floors, and a flooded basement are not adequate for God's Spirit. While these words are terms used to describe an actual building, they are applied here to represent the many worries, harmful habits and destructive memories that weaken and damage my spiritual home—my heart and mind. Using either reference for meaning, it doesn't measure up as my dream home.

Though these words describe the condition of a house with serious construction problems, a little imagination allows them to describe the results of my own careless planning and workmanship. Constructing an over-stuffed house crammed with troublesome tenants was not my original intention, but it's what I built. That's what happens when you try to build something without proper plans.

The Spirit gave me a way to look at myself honestly, much like Paul did for those Corinthians and has shown me that I don't have to be the way I have been. He has shown me that change is possible if that is what I want, and I don't have to do it alone. Like a run-down house can be renovated and made excitingly new and fully functional again, so can my heart and mind—my soul. Already there has been a clean up. Looks like the real work is about to begin.

While I can see that the Spirit has offered to advise and help in the project, it is also obvious that I need some training to do my part.

The training manual, and the blueprints, come from the architect—God—and are supplied in the form of the Bible.

I think the project and my apprenticeship are under way.

Has anybody seen my tape measure?

Debris That's Not to Be
discerning the harmful stuff

Ephesians 4:7–16

My reading time today finds me ready to move on, with a better understanding of why this renovation is needed and how it will happen. The verses refer to purpose and potential and remind me of previous passages in which Paul the missionary taught about the many parts necessary to make one whole body. He again mentions here, referring now to each of us, the value and purpose we have to each other. It appears that God's design intends for our teaching and help to come not only from prayer times with the Spirit but also through the Spirit's presence in each other. I'm not sure how that will come about, though it does remind me of my co-worker who has continued to offer encouragement to me when others seemed wary of my changing attitude.

This is not easy to understand, yet as I think about it a warm flush of rightness washes over me. I realize that I am not alone. Contrary to my father's opinion, I have learned that I am loved and valued, unconditionally, without ever needing to do something to deserve it.

The renovation has begun. All such projects are well-know for the mess and interruption they bring with them. Again using the vocabulary of the house metaphor, the interruptions I must contend with will be the many habits of thought and deed that I have given priority in the past, without questioning their worth. They would be represented as plenty of broken plaster, splintered wood, worn floorboards, frayed electrical wiring, and rusty pipes. The noise produced will be from the emotional struggle of me grappling with the process of removing them. The cover of dust on everything will represent the doubt and hesitation I continue to contribute to the project. Before the new services or materials can be installed, the old must be removed. Such debris is a natural result of renovation work. After the removal, progress is slower as I have to evaluate each removed piece and decide whether it should be reused, recycled or relegated to the dumpster. While awaiting judgment, this growing mound of debris gets in the way and is almost more difficult to deal with than when each piece was out of sight. There they were easier to ignore for a while at least. Now, all of these parts—good, bad, and in between—are mentally spread out in the open where I can't avoid looking at them. There are a large number of pieces that need to be held up for evaluation against the benchmarks offered in readings from the Bible.

At this point, I know what I don't want to do—but at the same time I'm unsure of exactly what I *am* going to do. It's an odd situation in which I'm not very comfortable. I am unable to move around freely without tripping over something. Choices are scattered everywhere and I need to clear up the area by deciding which items are designated as garbage. Once that stage is complete, the site will be ready for new construction.

Coming to that decision requires a lot of honest yet difficult appraisal. God's gentle Spirit has helped me identify these areas and given me the much-needed support to remain positive about myself even though I'm concentrating on the less desirable facets of my personality. In fact, the Spirit has served me much the way a hard-working apprentice would on a construction site. The Spirit has done everything possible to help but the initiative and actual decision to tackle each task is my choice. Those are my responsibility. Options, directions, and resources become available once my choices are made. At no time am I ever magically given the right choice or forced in a particular direction. At no time is the task automatically accomplished for me. It has occasionally been my wish that it could be, but I realize that shortcuts will not work.

I want to grow past those impulsive, selfish responses that have always been characteristic of me. Paul's writings encourage me and indicate that Christ has prepared others who will also help me at some stage of the project.

Hopefully, there is a big dumpster bin ready for me to fill up.

Dumpster

hanging on to the familiar

GALATIANS 5:13–15, 22–26

The apostle Paul wrote the letter I'm reading from today—Galatians—and I wish I could speak directly to him right now. I would like to ask him if he knew how deeply his words would reach into my heart and mind so many centuries after his writing them.

The words themselves can be found in any common dictionary, and by today's standards they might not even be considered particularly reflective. Something deeper is at work. It must be the power of God's Spirit working in Paul then, and in me now.

I continually use the term "heart" instead of "mind" because of my newfound realization that my awareness and understanding has more than an intellectual basis. While a lot of my learning about God is an exercise and function of my brain, I am receiving the most profound knowledge in another part of me, a part which my limited vocabulary has to label "heart."

Regardless of whether messages coming to me are visually or verbally initiated, they are granted a very different reception in my heart than in my mind. I have only noticed this distinction since the arrival of the Holy Spirit. I do not know if this is a new capacity or whether it has always existed but sat dormant.

The writers and speakers I'm encountering in the Bible always deliver wonderful, incisive illumination, usually with the same words I ridiculed so harshly for their silliness prior to meeting the guy in the white shirt—Jesus.

Something has obviously changed. I can only conclude that the "something" changing is me.

Change can be disturbing. By its very nature, change lacks familiarity. It infers movement to something untried and unknown. This is not a comfortable thought. Prior to this, had someone just appeared in front of my face declaring, "You need to change yourself" I would have made it quite clear that the suggestion was not welcome and might even have offered, depending on his attitude, to change the shape of his nose. Had it come from a church person, my response would have most definitely been less than polite. My first encounter with Jesus would certainly have aroused even greater resistance had he challenged me openly with the risk of change. I certainly wanted change—but in the circumstances and people around me—not in myself.

Since that introduction, however, each day has furthered the renovation process in me. The act of renovating is about making a house more functional, attractive, and updating its services to current code. It's about change, but the change is about improvement.

I admit I feel hesitant and have moments of doubt because it is all so unfamiliar to me. Thirty six days ago I didn't really believe God existed, let alone could touch my life this way. Something is happening to me and I want it to continue. Now, after just getting over the hurdle of my disbelief I am also becoming acutely aware of how undeserving I am of what is being given to me. In fact, as my understanding of the gift grows, so does my ability to see myself from a more honest vantage point. The view I behold is rarely good, even by the least discerning standards. Many times, what I see of my personality leaves me uncomfortable and ashamed. Surprisingly, as burdensome and unpleasant as that sounds, I have found it has not added any emotional weight to my life. As I come to value this opportunity to recognize my less than desirable characteristics, I feel grateful, albeit in the same awkward way as I am when someone warns me of my morning breath.

The reason for my gratitude is that I am now aware of a way for me to change my condition. I want to avail myself of it quickly. Over the past few weeks the boarder helped me realize the need to "clean house" of the inner clutter of old hurts, anger, and guilt that piled up over the years. I had never done that before. Sorting through my memories and attitudes, I was surprised by how much useless, even hazardous junk I have accumulated. Readings from the Bible in recent weeks have come to mind, their lessons providing labels for the boxes of attitudes, memories, attractions, habits, and relationships that have been crammed into the corners of my being and are affecting my life. Some are positive but far too many are negative.

The labels made the task of sorting easier by correctly identifying many things I had not given much thought to, though I admit these boxes sometimes surprised me. Some boxes I was reluctant to throw away, though I know I really shouldn't be. My boarder let me skip by them upon seeing my reaction and moved on to the next corner. There was lots to sort through and, in spite of the large number of items I decided to get rid of, a number of things remained.

Today, Paul directs my attention to some of the boxes I kept. It's like I'm standing in the sun on the stone-paved courtyard where he addressed a group of men and women in Galatians 5. His attention moves through the faces before him, from one to the next, and then finally holds his gaze on me. He points to my load of boxes and asks, "*Why are you keeping all of those?*" His tone isn't accusatory, but instead resonates with genuine concern. "*Why do you want to continue holding that anger? Why do you still want to keep that hurtful memory? Why are you afraid of love?*" His questions indicate his care for my well-being. I can't ignore his concern for me nor do I want to.

Maybe I need to make a few more trips to the dumpster.

Search & Rescue
lost is not the intention, help is available

PSALM 139:1–5

The words of the Psalms I have read so far are uncanny in how accurately they express my thoughts and feelings and answer my questions. They even answer the questions I feel but cannot phrase. They calm my troubled thoughts and somehow reassure me that I am safe and not alone. As a result, they provide me with generous refills of the proof I still need about God's presence in my life.

I guess I am like Thomas, the last disciple to see Jesus after his return to life. The other disciples told Thomas the breathtaking news that Jesus was back, but he refused to believe it. Thomas needed to see and touch the wounds inflicted during the crucifixion. He needed proof. The theoretical and practical preparation he had received was not enough for him to simply believe.

If I am right in assuming that he and I are alike, I also know he needed his belief topped up at regular intervals just like I do. I need moments of reassurance, and the words of Psalm 139 certainly do that.

Since my initial rescue, I have been given explanations of the help I am receiving and understanding about the cause of the problems I face. There has been a constant flow of proof given to me, and most often it has been through reading a verse or two like this. The comfort and direction I am finding in the Bible are so intimately specific that it feels like it was written just for me.

But how can that be?

A significant number of people and languages were involved in recording all that is written in the Bible, and many more individuals translated those words into various languages. As if this wasn't complicated enough, the entire process was spread across a time span of several millennia before it was completed. Most people today would conclude that it is impossible to retain accuracy and the intent of even a single story under such circumstances. Given all the potential for failure, it seems improbable that those stories could relate to me so personally and perfectly.

When I was a Boy Scout, our troop played a game where the leader would whisper a short story to the first scout seated in a group forming a circle. The scout in turn whispered it to the boy beside him. This continued around the circle until the last one stood up and repeated the story as it was told to him. Ideally, it was supposed to be the same as the original. Though sometimes providing hilarious moments, it was intended as a serious exercise designed to develop comprehension and an accurate memory. The context of this skill-building exercise was to simulate a rescue operation initiated by the international distress call, "Mayday, Mayday, Mayday."

Needless to say, it was a difficult task. Sometimes the Scout leader would insert himself into the circle at intermittent points to correct any errors or omissions, but when he didn't the result was a woefully inadequate message. Had it been an actual emergency, someone would have been in a lot of trouble.

I see a parallel to this game in the Bible.

God wanted to provide us with the information we need to survive and grow as we live our lives. The One who created us knows how best to guide and restore us. Good communication with God is absolutely necessary, but it appears that it is our choice whether to employ it or not. It makes sense that if God imposed this communication on us it would remove our free will and that reduces us to puppets on a string.

God's story of creation and relationship began as experience and narrative. It was passed along from person to person, and generation to generation, for a long period of time before there was any form of physical documentation. The story expanded as it was experienced and understood by more people. Obviously its intention is to guide us as it describes the creator to the created. As the story passed along, it recorded the numerous times God sent someone to ensure the story remained intact and understandable, just as the Scout leader did for us. Those prophets and leaders became essential, integral parts of the story that is referred to as the Word of God—the Bible.

History records how God's Word has been misunderstood, misconstrued, and ignored in spite of the prophets God sent. God's concern for us resulted in the incredible physical appearance on earth of the Christ in the person of Jesus.

At the beginning of the Bible, God tells us that we are created in his likeness. Through Jesus we can see and hear what that means for us. Jesus was inserted into the human storyline to once again correct the message and remove the risk inherent in our tendency to misinterpret or ignore it. Jesus became the Word of God in flesh and blood.

At the end of Jesus' time here, the Holy Spirit of God came to fill the role as guardian of the story in a personal manner for each individual who sought and welcomed this contact. This Spirit form of God guided many women and men to gather, record, translate, protect, live, and distribute God's message through the physical, political, spiritual, and intellectual obstacles they encountered. Somewhere along the line, the collected recordings became known as the Bible. Its purpose is to comfort and guide us as we navigate this life and introduce us to an incredible relationship with our Creator.

It seems the Spirit's role is much like that of the Scout leader, ensuring that everyone has the opportunity to hear the correct story. Not everyone listens, though.

I know people who try to understand the Bible only with their intellect and thus see it as a document of contradiction and antiquity, void of personal relevance. Their rebuttals of its accuracy, judged through the filter of their own logic, can be vigorous. Their judgments are often influenced by common opinion or negative life circumstances that have not been resolved. Few people make a serious effort to discover what the Bible is until faced with a life crisis. It embarrasses me to think that I too, have been one of those people.

I have seen other people who listen to the Bible's message but hear only its condemnation of selfish acts and resent its call to change. Its message of righteousness, its indictment of greed, and its call for justice threaten their small circle of comfortable indulgence. Needless to say, these people reject it as well and miss the wealth it offers.

But there are also many people who hear the message of the Bible and recognize it as a signal beacon, reaching to each generation across the distance of time, logic and pride. It marks a clear course through the obstacles of life. These people respond to its wisdom and become beacons themselves for others as the Spirit works through them.

The Bible recounts many distress calls, but is itself a rescue response. Those who go to it in need soon find themselves able to hear and understand the Bible in their heart. It guarantees the rescue of spirit and body for every person who comes to it, regardless of the details of their need or their sense of worthiness. Its powerful message of love is like an A535 rub down to an aching heart or mind. Its personalized perfection must be due to the fact that God knows each of us individually and intimately through the Holy Spirit. The stories of the Bible demonstrate that understanding and offer words of comfort and guidance to us.

We are valued and loved by God, who wants to rescue us—as long as we want to be rescued.

Are You There?
present 24/7

PSALM 139:1–18

This Psalm is on the list again, though with a few more verses added. It was written by David, the great king I mentioned earlier. I almost skip it, because I don't see how anything different can come to me from it. However I decide to proceed according to the plan.

My attention quickly focuses on the lines about the days of my life being known to God and recorded before I was even born. I don't like this.

My mind quickly loads up video reruns of the frightening and hurtful times I have gone through while my heart remembers the aches. If they were known beforehand, why did God let them happen to me? What about all the other terrible things that have happened to women, children, and men throughout history and continue even now as I write these words? Does God do these things to us deliberately?

I sit for a long time, thinking about this. Anger and fear hover close by, trying to break through the fragile net of trust I have managed to weave.

I think of Job, a man I came across when looking up names a while ago. His story is told in an Old Testament book of the same name. It's a story of a man who faced a severe trial and examination of his faith in God. I found and read it and it appeared to be an unfair test in which the teacher wants to dismiss the student's achievements and crush his confidence. By the end of the story, however, the test actually gave Job the opportunity to separate the thoughts and actions of his own will from those of God. He was able to see whether his response to God was only based on the benefits he was receiving or if it had real depth and he was indeed a changed person because of his relationship with God.

But God keeps professing and giving so much love to us—why such a harsh test?

If the statement in this Psalm is correct, then God already knew how genuine Job's faith was. It doesn't say, however, that God decided beforehand what Job or I would do with our lives. The account says only that God knew our lives before we lived them. So what is going on?

I decide to reread Job's story, and in doing so I notice an important detail overlooked in my first reading. God did not devise the test. Satan did.

Satan is a character I have not spent much time learning about. Most of my knowledge has been formed from television and movies. No doubt such a knowledge base is inadequate, and probably even misguided, but one thing is consistent in biblical and public perceptions—Satan's purpose is absolutely opposite to God's. In many instances throughout the Bible we are warned of the ever-present danger Satan is to us. Like many of the nursery rhyme characters we read about however, we often ignore the warnings. Fortunately, God stays close by when we wander into the dark and dangerous corners of life.

If the example of Job is a model for me, I can now have the confidence of knowing every time I face a trial that it is an opportunity for me to make choices reflecting whether I am listening to God or not. Using the illustration of a school test again, once the results are handed back, I will know where I stand and my confidence should grow. In this way, God preserves my freedom to make my own choices. I can change my direction at any time. Caution is warranted though, because I am also free to make mistakes, and therefore must learn how to make good choices and accept responsibility for the bad ones.

In spite of what a lot of people wish then, it seems that God doesn't interfere with the unfolding of free will or natural consequences, changing every bad thing that could happen. This Psalm makes it very clear though that God is always present. Not knowing this or perhaps even denying it doesn't alter that fact.

While David has impressed me with his ability to understand what God has shown him, he also displays his inner feelings when he exclaims how incredible and complex he finds the extent of God's presence and how impossible it is to understand how God works.

I heartily agree, for I am constantly amazed by how infinite the completeness of God's care for each of us is. It goes well beyond my capability to understand, let alone explain. Every detail is so exact and perfect that it produces exquisite delight and awe when discovered and recognized.

In this day's reading, I come to realize how much confidence and trust I have developed in God since this odyssey began. Before, when confronted by something I did not understand, my disbelief formed an obstacle so impermeable that I felt unable to grasp the solution, so I gave up. Lately, I realize that those obstacles are gateways of doubt that I can learn to open.

I now want to pass through those gates. While I don't want difficult or hurtful situations in my life or anyone else's, I can see the creative potential in them that either God or I can use. They are opportunities to look honestly at my needs and motivations. This explains the stories told of people who enter a lonely hotel room, devoid of hope, perhaps even on the brink of desperate action, yet later leave that same room overflowing with hope and promise because of an encounter with God and the Holy Spirit through a Bible found in a dresser drawer. Those who have done so, along with David and me, have learned that God will never, under any circumstance, leave us alone and unprotected. Those times when we feel most alone and hopeless are when God can be the closest to us.

I agree with David when he writes that there is no place we can go to escape God's presence—but now I think that is a promise, not a threat.

Eviction Notices
deep-seated attitudes and habits

EPHESIANS 5:15–21

am switching my time with the paperback Bible to mornings to make this the
first thing I do every day. Today is already going to be a test though because
my mind is crammed with a myriad of family concerns and work demands.
Fortunately after a brief struggle my temptation to just get on with the day and
skip my reading time lost. What this time does for me is too valuable to miss.

Today's reading from Ephesians starts with warnings about the way you live
and the company you keep. It makes a very clear declaration that unless you are
trying to discern what God wants to give you in life, you are living foolishly and
will be easily swallowed by the circumstances around you.

My serenity is elbowed here by images of the Mad Parade and the chaotic
Boarding House. The difference between those times and now is incredible.
The days when I drifted away from dedicating time to prayer, I was quickly
absorbed again by the brusque turbulence of life and circumstances. I don't need
to contemplate Paul's words very long to understand their truth. I wonder if he
knew the extent to which it is possible to be drawn into and often battered by
those circumstances.

Paul goes on to encourage us to drink in the Holy Spirit rather than filling up
on wine. This analogy causes me to compare those times of celebration when my
alcohol consumption led to impaired thinking versus my moments of celebration
with the Spirit, in which my thinking was clear and amplified.

Today's lesson reminds me to offer thanks to God for everything. I doubt this is a lesson in etiquette so much as a reminder to be conscious of habitually being so busy enjoying myself—or, conversely, moping in self-pity—that I fail to notice all that God provides for me. As these sessions lift the screen of unfocused and cluttered thinking, I begin to see that God has always been concerned with my life. My own logic and stubbornness have kept me from seeing this in the past.

The accumulation of bad results from my own choices and life's evolving circumstances added to the debris blocking my view of God. My old attitude and self-serving choices have built an immense hoarding that covered the construction site of my temple. The purpose of those plywood and steel fence enclosures is to cover and protect passersby from construction activity, not to keep the builder out, as I was doing.

It has taken a long time for me to even vaguely understand what I have done to myself. Until recently, I didn't think I had any reasons to be thankful, let alone a God to thank. But at this moment, I am almost overwhelmed by a desire to thank God. I am so thankful that these timeless stories from God are true. I am so thankful that God is real and wants a relationship with me—in spite of everything I have done wrong and everything I should have done but failed to do.

I even embrace the last sentence of today's reading, which directs us to submit ourselves to each other because of Christ. Earlier, we were asked to submit to the Spirit's lead. My customary reaction to such a thought would be rejection, because giving in to others meant I was weak—bondage would result and others would look on me with disdain.

Surprisingly, my reaction now is not my old one. I realize that my insistence on independent thinking and acting can be selfish and dangerous. For me, it led to pride and foolishness and my ignorance mistook them for strength and knowledge. The fruit this attitude has born in my life is more like the meagre, scabby apples from a neglected roadside tree than the red treat traditionally given to teachers.

Jesus' call for submission is gently opening me, revealing the freedom of life it produces.

The paradox that freedom can be had in submission does not escape me, but instead of rejection it tickles my curiosity to understand it better. I am so thankful for what is happening.

The more I learn—the fewer disruptive tenants I have yet to kick out of the Boarding House.

Team Leader
the perfect example

MATTHEW 28:19–20

Recorded in today's reading are the last words Jesus spoke to the remaining eleven disciples—Judas Iscariot no longer amongst them—before physically leaving the world. These words are the instructions that guided their work, eventually resulting in the establishment of the Christian church. They would be almost innocuous if not for the startling fact that Jesus spoke them *after* his death.

I try to empathize with what this small group would have been thinking and feeling as Jesus spoke to them. Emotionally at this point they must have had a sense of being turned upside-down.

In a rapid-fire sequence of events, this man had called them away from the safe routine of their daily lives, told them incredible things about God, taught them how to live a life of confidence and abundance as they brought healing to hurting people, shared a loving and dependable friendship with them like no other they had ever experienced, and then was arrested, tried, convicted, and put to death.

This peaceful man, who spoke only of loving and serving others, who took nothing for himself, who performed breathtaking miracles that brought wholeness back into warped limbs, unseeing eyes, and lifeless bodies, and even made stupendous claims about living forever if you followed him, had now himself been allowed to die.

Only three days after his death, while this small group of people still reeled from the shock of their loss and its puzzling contradictions, they were further assaulted, first by stories of the disappearance of his body, and then by reports of his being seen alive by Mary Magdalene, Joanna, and Mary, the mother of James and Jesus. These women also told of having seen and been spoken to by an angel. It must have been bizarre for them.

In less than two weeks, the group was subjected to a spectrum of emotions, witnessing two parades featuring Jesus as the central focus. At the first one, they shared the pride and joy of his triumphant entry into the city of Jerusalem as he was hailed a great prophet and healer by the crowds lining the streets to see him. Then they watched a second, grim parade in which this beloved man— who was variously their leader, son, brother, and friend—was led to his gruesome execution. Following the execution, they nervously huddled in an apartment for some time, fearful that the authorities would seek them out. Then, over the next few weeks, Jesus appeared before them several times in their small groups of twos and threes, proving that his life somehow existed beyond death, just as he had told them it would.

Jesus' core team of Peter, John, the two Jameses, Andrew, Philip, Thomas, Bartholomew, Matthew, Simon, and James' son—who also bore the name Judas—was meeting in response to his instructions on a country hillside. These eleven, embraced by a warm breeze and the sweet fragrance of grass and wild flowers, looked at him and listened to his voice. He was with them again.

It is easy to assume that they were overwhelmed with joy, excitedly speculating on what they would do next. These people lived in a country that was occupied by a brutal military power. They were probably expecting this to be the moment long dreamed of by the generations before them, and which they, too, had envisioned as children, rapturously listening to stories their parents told them about the Messiah who was to come to their rescue. Surely now he would announce plans to lead them into political victory and freedom. Now all the injustices suffered by their people would be righted, and maybe even avenged.

Instead, as their emotions were lifted up, his words announced his imminent departure. What a wild roller coaster ride their emotions must have been on! They didn't know it yet, but the peace they were to achieve would extend far beyond what could be achieved through political strategies and negotiation.

Imagining myself in their place fills me with confusion, anger, doubt, and even fear. Why doesn't he save himself? How can he share so much with us and then leave like this? How can I do as he asks without him being here? If even he had to suffer so much, what awaits me? These questions must have been on their lips, too.

Christ's first sentences in today's reading demonstrate his absolute focus and commitment to the job at hand. The team has to assume new responsibilities because the team leader is moving up to head office. Jesus restates their mandate and the authority they work under, reminding them of the extensive preparation they have had for what lies ahead. God wants the world's people to know of their Creator's existence and love for them, and how that knowledge can transform their lives.

He gives them straight talk. He had a job to do, people to train and motivate. He had done it and now it was time for him to leave and for them to get on with their assignment. He knew his team. He knew their capabilities even better than they did. He was confident of their success and demonstrated this by voicing his expectation of their success in spite of his physical absence. He was a leader who always worked with them, developing their abilities and encouraging them to achieve their best. His pushing, prodding, teaching, encouragement, and example had changed their lives and prepared them to go out and do the same for other people. Approximately three years of intensive training had been given to these men and women as they lived and traveled together with him. Through him they had seen God in a way no other people ever had.

But if those disciples were anything like me, in spite of all they had, at that moment their self-confidence was nowhere in sight. Jesus understood that hesitance and their temptation not to push ahead. In recognition of this and his commitment to his co-workers, he delivered his last sentence—not words of instruction or chastisement, but comfort and assurance as, in his last physical moments on earth, he again served his servants in their needs and reminded them he will always be with them through all time and everything that lies ahead.

These words are proof again of his great understanding and gentle nature. They do not fit our stereotypical image of male authority. His teachings always speak of love and compassion, yet they are not those of a flaky, wide-eyed dreamer. He was a bold activist. The few stories I now know about him show him to be passionately involved and committed, undaunted and ready for action. The love he spoke of was certainly not romanticism or limited to lip service. His type of love resulted in healing and building for those who held and received it. He wanted his disciples to exemplify that same love.

He was leaving them, though he revealed that even in his physical absence he was committed to continuing his presence with them. It was a critical moment for his followers. Christ knew that their temporal nature could limit their belief, causing them to stumble over or dismiss those times and circumstances that would go beyond human reason. He knew the disciples would need this charge and promise from him in order to break through the ensnaring nets of logic and doubt. As further evidence of his absolute understanding of humanity, his last spoken words were a reassurance to them—and us, today—of his presence and faith. He was giving them the conviction they would need to move ahead and confidently challenge fearful times when it would be a lot easier to turn back.

Marvelling at what is being shown to me, my thoughts return to a still picture of Jesus amongst this group of people. Though from my perspective he was the leader and should therefore have expected certain privileges and respect, it strikes me that he was the most humble of them all. He served them in a way that was uniquely and fully satisfying to each individual. Every one of them had become more whole by following him.

While relishing the warmth of this thought, the setting changes from a motionless tableau as he turns and looks over to me, smiling an acknowledging invitation.

"Follow me."

Thermometer
self awareness and self control

2 TIMOTHY 2:22–26

Confrontation has been one of my most consistent forms of interaction with other people. Fatigue from the ever-present pulling and shoving within me has resulted in hard-edged sharpness when I deal with people.

Everyone meets that barrage when encountering me, whether they are family members, friends, or strangers. I vent the frustration and anger I feel towards myself and a world that seems unaware and uncaring of me. When, where, and upon whom I administer these blistering expletives are immaterial to me. Unfortunately, rather than producing the relief I seek, these outbursts usually add new weight to my already heavy load.

Those who stand and meet my challenges head-on feel the impact of my self-destructive fury. After a couple of attempts, they don't bother trying anymore. The ones who offer softness earn only scorn when my abuse forces them into retreat. I recall in particular the individuals who have pointed me to God as a source of help. They have invariably seen the worst of the maelstrom within me.

Discomfort and embarrassment accompany these recollections as my new tenant guides me through the message of today's Bible reading. I have hurt and rejected a lot of people, and though it has not been as harsh as usual lately, I feel the sting of another such encounter as I head to my prayer time today.

These verses offer specific teaching about the attitude and behaviour of those who would be followers of Jesus. They warn that without successfully learning these lessons, we are vulnerable to evil's trap. My emotional temperature soars as images flash through my mind of an animal frantically twisting, pulling, and gnawing to escape from a leg trap. They are revolting sights of extreme desperation, but at the moment I see a clear parallel between those critters and me. Having never consciously sought, much less exercised, such traits as taught in the Bible, I am unprepared and therefore caught in this trap, which ensnares the spirit, if not the body. This disturbing realization produces a frightening image of myself.

Somewhat surprising, though, is the distinct sense of hope that also comes to me upon reading these verses. What is being given here is the method of release from such contraptions. Struggling does not work. Anger, strength, and expletives do not undo the trap. If this lesson is true, learning about and striving for righteousness, faith, love, and peace are the mechanisms for finding freedom and avoiding arguments and demeaning confrontations. Talk about personalized messages! This one shows me why I feel as though I am always travelling in painful circles.

The lesson doesn't stop there. The reading also indicates that there are others who call to God for help. Almost like a homework assignment, I'm instructed to gather with these others in order to seek freedom. The concluding words proffer promise of both liberty and the privilege of responsibility. They state that the student acquiring freedom through this knowledge can one day bring release to others.

I speak aloud to my boarder about the unexpectedness of this teaching and how perfectly it fits me. After inviting the Spirit to move in, I expected to appreciate and accept religious and mystical matters, but I did not expect this. Here I am receiving practical understanding of the consequences of my choices.

My quiet but extraordinary companion chuckles softly and offers a silent suggestion to use this Bible lesson as a thermometer. A thermometer? After a few puzzling minutes, I realize that I can, in fact, visualize my emotional state as temperature. It seems to me that everyone around me is usually in a calm and comfortable temperature zone. In contrast, my customary internal turmoil registers much higher, uncomfortable temperatures. When I am upset and angry, my temperature goes up. When exploding at someone or something, it reaches feverish height.

Interestingly, using this analogy and reflecting on the time since these encounters with the Holy Spirit began, my average temperature has been considerably lower. Only on those infrequent occasions when I allow myself to slip back into old habits and attitudes does it rise. I have made progress.

I'm curious about what this faith can do.

My fever appears to be broken.

Lawn Care

healthy spiritual living

Matthew 13:1–23

I am getting a bit more involved with the life of my family and friends again. It has been such a liberating opportunity for me to join in the activities around me with a fresh attitude and perspective. I feel whole and alive again. Life in the Boarding House, amongst the tools and supplies, continues to improve.

This lightness of heart and mind comes from knowing that not only is God real, but Jesus loves me and somehow his Holy Spirit is right here with me. It feels like I'm in a sequence from a Disney family film where those magical moments let you feel that life really is a great adventure to be enjoyed.

During my recent encounters, I have been able to touch this lightness of life. The moments often evaporate shortly after though, when they're exposed to the reality of my routine in a world that wants to ignore God. This time, they have not. My load has been lifted from me and I am enjoying everything and everyone.

Last night an unexpected encounter with a member of the Mad Parade brought back chilling memories of the crippling harassment it exerted on my life.

At my introduction to the Mad Parade, I was unaware of the danger of listening to those parade members who coaxed me along with attractive promises. As I yielded to images of the good times they painted, my pride and self-centredness grew. Eventually, like the people spoken of in verses 20 to 22, things went wrong. Almost imperceptibly, the counterfeit self confidence I was developing shape-shifted into a confrontational attitude, which in turn led to conflict and confusion, and finally produced a slow, battered sense of being lost. This awareness of defeat shaped only one possibility, that of a final exit from it all—from life itself.

These verses recall the hard soil yard pocked with patches of spiky grass in front of the first image of that pathetic boarding house.

I'm anxious to get on with the renovation job.

This parable of the sown seeds, warns me to be careful —that it won't be easy. I must pay attention to the one who provided the key to my cell not so long ago. My freedom from the cell of the restricted, burdened personality I had become is not intended to be a single bolt-to-freedom escape. Just as popular stories of heroic escapes from prisoner-of-war camps illustrate, preparation and vigilance are critical for success, because there are many obstacles awaiting the escapee.

I am thankful that my boarder is showing me the necessity of developing prayer as a daily part of my life. It is not just a panic button to be punched in emergencies. As I read, the analogy of the rocky soil's inadequacy for sustaining life becomes discomfortingly relevant for me.

My awareness of God, Jesus, and the Holy Spirit—and the insights I've been given in the process of my introduction to them—has been welcomed by my intellect and spirit like soft soil welcomes new seeds. After an initial hesitant gestation period, the seed—the acceptance of the reality of God—popped open and a new plant—faith—began to grow. But am I going to work hard enough for it to mature and change my life?

That is what I want to happen. I want this faith to grow in me, and like the crops in the parable I want it to produce an abundant yield through the actions of my life each day. It seems the way to do that is stick with the paperback Bible, my scribbler notebook and the Spirit. The renovation needs to continue.

In the context of the Boarding House, I need a whole lawn not just spotty patches of green and brown.

A Shepherd in the House
guidance, comfort and help

1 JOHN 3:1–3

On the outside, it's still pretty much the same face greeting me in the bathroom mirror every morning. The frown is a little less dominant though and on the inside things are definitely different. I know each day is going to bring contact with Jesus through His Spirit again, and that will bring another sponge bath of freedom. A sense of excitement and anticipation starts each day. I'm never sure what to expect—only that I will discover something new.

I remember a similar feeling from the childhood games of tag I played at dusk on a summer evening. We ran in and out of driveways and side yards, hopping fences and squeezing through small openings, encouraged by adjoining properties without fences, never knowing for sure what we would encounter as we breathlessly rounded the next turn but exhilarated by the risk rather than restrained by it. That's how I feel about these times of dialogue through the Bible readings. Each time is an adventure.

The metaphor of the boarding house allows me to better see myself and understand my troubled thoughts. The unsynchronized schedules of the various tenants are colliding a little less frequently. My times in prayer and reading are providing a refreshing calm space in which to think about my actions and feelings, past and present.

I realize there are still disturbing characters present who can and do send me scurrying back to safer places, but there are also more and larger safe areas since inviting that last boarder, the Spirit. I know it sounds illogical, but bringing into my mind a new framework of thinking is actually lightening my mental and emotional load rather than straining its capacity.

So, what about this new boarder? He's never in my way, yet always present when I need him. He's always ready to sit and listen to me, always willing to duck my abusive retorts. I never fail to be welcomed with understanding and comfort. Patience greets my stubbornness and self-pity. Ever-present, too, is the challenge to taste the difference between the life I lived and the life offered through the Bible.

In fact, this boarder is becoming my best friend.

He has no visible form, but I his presence is quite tangible. In lighter moments, such as while lathering behind the shower curtain, I wonder again about his ability to see me. My embarrassment initially had me concerned about my unclothed state. After a few moments of assessment, however, I realized that my embarrassment came more from being concerned about my physical nakedness needing to be hidden from this God who could see much more—into the often dark thoughts of my heart and mind.

Though I am able to picture other physical moments when I would rather that no one else be able to watch, exposure of my thoughts tops the list of things that would warrant the most embarrassment. No physical exposure could be more uncomfortable than having my thoughts seen openly.

My new companion has come to me with a wholeness that encompasses the very best that I know about feminine and masculine characteristics, including something extra I am unable to capture and contain in words. Privacy and concealment from this person of God is absolutely unnecessary, even though openness forces me to look at those actions and thoughts I would prefer to hide. On several occasions, this awareness of being seen has prompted me to respond to situations differently than I otherwise would have. It is uncomfortable to respond at first, but feels great when I allow it to change my course of thought or action to something positive.

With my awareness of this change in the back of my mind, I'm excited by John's words today, which tell me I am loved so much by God that I am actually to be called one of God's children. By knowing this and hoping in this, I will be able to keep myself pure. Now there's an adjective I would never have thought could be used to describe me—pure.

I catch an inference here that people who do not understand that they are creations of God, and instead live their lives in the limited hope allowed by human knowledge and wisdom, are missing a large part of their potential for life and freedom.

Reflecting on my unique experience to this point reminds me that only since I've started listening to the Spirit have I started to feel the excitement of hope. Each time I have accepted the knowledge or insight given to me, I have had an ever-deepening understanding and ever-increasing thirst for more. The more I learn about Christ's message, the greater is my sense of freedom.

This freedom seems incongruent with what I thought it would be like to be obedient to a lot of rules and laws from a powerful ruler somewhere in the sky.

When first pushed into this experience—though now I am viewing it as a pull to rescue rather than a forceful drag into custody—I was given something I had not specifically requested. Now, the more I get, the more I want. It is like something inside me had been turned off and is now turned on.

I want to discover and do what God wants for me instead of what I think I want. This is resulting in a sense of freedom I have never experienced before. I am happier. I have greater calmness and self-control. There is a little less internal chaos.

My faded mental images from Sunday school stories are restored to full colour as I remember Jesus talking about anything being possible to those who have faith. Also repainted are the pictures I formed in my mind when I first learned Psalm 23—adventure comic strip images of a robed figure guarding me as I walk along dangerous trails, past dark shadowy figures, feasting at a table filled with delicacies while people I once thought could keep me away from such happiness look on in envy.

I realize that these trails, shadows, and enemies, though they do not resemble my childhood visualizations, are very real, just as they were for the writer of Psalm 23 so long ago. I can't write inspiring poetic phrases like those, but I do know that the same loving God who rescued, guided, and provided for that person has now come to rescue me.

Just as the childhood images of my enemies are not the same as the reality of my adulthood, Jesus' representation simply as a robed shepherd is not appropriate, either. I have enemies mostly internal and of my own making, but I also have a guide and protector.

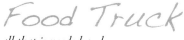

Food Truck

all that is needed and more

MARK 6:30–44

Before picking up the Bible today, I reflect for a few moments on all the incredible things I've learned since discovering prayer with God. I am no longer as entangled or weighed down by fear and uncertainty. Today I am experiencing the lightness that accompanies this new sense of freedom.

This raises the question "Freedom from what?"

The answer to that question has changed my life. The most easily noticed freedom I now enjoy is the absence of my overflowing, directionless anger. I don't worry as much as I did before. The incessant ricocheting of my thoughts and emotions has abated substantially and I no longer wrestle with the bed sheets and shadows on the walls before finding sleep at night. This experience is akin to being released from prison, though until my "flight" it was difficult to articulate what formed my prison. Since then, I know I want to stay close to the guy with the key ring. The twist is, he is not the jailer.

Today's verses immediately cause two incongruent thoughts to flash through my mind. First is the exhilaration once again of being free and the second is the welcome sound of a food truck horn pulling into a construction site mid morning.

They tell about a huge crowd of people who were determined to stay in the company of Jesus even after he had finished serving them and was seeking rest for himself. Had I been there, I would have joined them, not out of selfishness but because of the realization that Jesus has something so vital for life. The crowd was going to stick with him and get all that he was offering, now that they had sampled what he brought. In fact, the story makes clear that their determination was successful at interrupting Jesus and the disciples in their attempt to find a bit of quiet time to rest.

Obviously, the daily schedule of teaching and healing had been very busy. This passage records how physically and emotionally drained Jesus and his band were from their work in meeting the needs of the individuals who came to them. I can only speculate what those specific needs were, but I find it easy to believe many were seeking, as I am, release from the emotional, physical, and intellectual confines of their own logic and behaviour. Others probably needed relief from the weight of moral or sexual abuses. No doubt some, too, were grasping for relief from physical ailments, burdens, and the residual hopelessness resulting from their stress and anxiety.

No approved, patented medicines existed at that time, nor were there any highly educated and trained psychologists and surgeons available to them. Can we even begin to comprehend how they felt about this man and his followers who gave them all that and loved them, too? Here, in the affluent net of twenty-first century medicine and science, I have all of these luxuries and more. Still, I hadn't found the relief I needed until I met Jesus. No wonder this crowd followed him. No wonder I don't want to leave him.

On this occasion, in spite of his own tiredness, Jesus went beyond the incredible healing of minds and bodies and fed their hungry stomachs as well. Rather than giving them exactly what they were seeking—which was already miraculous and exceeded all reasonable expectations—and then sending them back to their own lives, he addressed their comfort and basic needs by providing a meal as well. In doing so, not only did he contradict all conventional logic in his method of providing something to eat, but he also did so in portions that far surpassed their need. This act by itself tells of the measure of Jesus' concern and compassion for people, to say nothing of his capacity to perform the impossible.

Logic brings us to an obvious conclusion: serving a satisfying dinner to five thousand people is no small catering feat, especially with no notice. This is no job for even the best street food vendor yet all Jesus held in his hand was a basket containing five loaves of bread and two fish.

The gathered crowd that day believed in him. Therefore, in his love he was able to give them far more than they needed or asked for. Christ, tired and at the end of a long day, looked beyond his own need. He had already provided healing for their physical ailments and the peace of mind they anxiously sought. He didn't need to prove anything more. But he cared for them. I am convinced he can and will do the same for us today. I may not have everything I want but I will have everything I need.

Nightfall was approaching, the people were hungry, and they were in a remote place far from their homes and eateries. They were happy and no doubt would have left, grateful for what they had received. They would have been able to survive their rumbling digestive systems. Jesus, though, acted on his concern for their comfort and, accepting the little food available to him, served them a meal so bountiful that the leftovers exceeded the amount of food he started with. I understand this to say, contrary to our scientific opinion, that it is ultimately not we ourselves but God who provides for us. We need to be responsible and do our part but we will benefit greatly if we can understand and have faith in it as it applies to our needs, as individuals and as a community.

Again I find myself identifying with the men and women who were present in the crowd that day. I, too, want to stay near this person who proves his care for each and every one of us with such fullness.

It is another incredible story that has to be seen in the light of what it is teaching. My sample nibbles have convinced me that this is no light lunch—I am invited to a banquet.

Home Alone
checking the progress

Hebrews 3:1–6

After yesterday's reading, this one captures my attention like a hard twist of the ear, as is usually the intention of such twists. The words here feel incredibly personal and deliver an ambiguous combination of comfort and query. Comfort, because I feel that this greeting to these faithful men includes me. Query is stirred upon reading the words "partners with those called to heaven."

A small yellow flag of caution waves on the display monitor of my mind. What does that phrase mean? I don't want to seem ungrateful or anything after being rescued from a very disruptive inner life, but now that I'm feeling better I'm hesitant about allowing myself to be drawn into something unknown. Does this greeting hint at some hidden clause or trap? I'm embarrassed to think this after all I've been given, but the thoughts are there. Am I now expected to become some kind of religious nut?

The Spirit, who by way of answer whisks me back to the Boarding House, accepts my querulous attitude. It's been a while since I've been here. What am I going to see this time?

We start with a casual walk around, as if returning from a holiday trip. Clamour and commotion excepted, everything appears to be as I last saw it. All is quiet, as though the tenants are out for the afternoon. Dropping into a comfortable chair in the well-used living room, I'm afforded the opportunity to absorb my surroundings. It's not as jammed and oppressive as before. What I do see, various pieces of furniture, wall hangings, and assorted memorabilia, bring a soft, nostalgic peace to my mind. It occurs to me that I was previously always too distracted by the clutter and hectic demand of daily circumstances to enjoy them.

I sit quietly for some time, enjoying each item and remembering the story of how it came to be there. Eventually my attention shifts though and I start to notice other objects claiming space on tabletops and shelves. Their presence is awkward, adding disarray. I think they've always been here. Some I recognize, others I do not. They have the appearance of being left by someone either too busy or uncaring to tidy up.

In response to this observation my boarder, the project manager, and I set out and retrace our initial tour through the house, upstairs and down. In each room we visit, I notice more artifacts of untidiness carelessly strewn about. Some rooms have more than others. The attic and basement, for example, make an art form of this largesse. I'm staggered by their numbers. Why have I saved them all, and where have those which I do not remember acquiring come from?

Returning to the well-worn living room chair, the Spirit prompts me to reread the excerpt from the letter to the Hebrews. It describes faithfulness in building a house and the honour given to the builder. It ends by indicating that Christians are the house of God that Christ is building.

Dim lights flicker in my mind as I associate those words with the clutter in the Boarding House. The feeling of a smile from my companion warms me— usually a sign that my search for the right answer is getting warmer.

The now familiar sensation of a new discovery tingles within me. Here I am in the Boarding House again, quiet and cluttered as it is. The Holy Spirit has already coached me into the realization that it represents my inner life— the source of my thoughts, feelings, and resulting attitudes. It is quiet today and I'm able to look closely at its contents without interruption. The Hebrews verses, focused on house building, remind me of another understanding I have gained—that of each of us being temples for the Holy Spirit.

I have built the Boarding House—including all its clamour, confusion, and clutter. Not everything is as I expected or wanted it to be, and certainly it is far from what it could be. The building is an honest and predictable result of my approach and methods of construction. Since that night when I answered the doorbell and invited Christ in, the Spirit has been helping me see the house for what it is. My understanding is that reorganization and renovation can only happen with my agreement and will only continue as long as the task is what I want.

Many times, I have been perplexed by the possibility and process of everything I have experienced. Without the visual metaphor of the Boarding House, it is impossible for me to understand these changes in my thoughts and feelings. On one point, however, I stand convinced—I am feeling more peaceful as these subtle changes occur and can only describe the sensation as being one of healing.

When Jesus came to me, he came to a worn and battered house. It was full of problems, from its haphazard contents and lack of proper maintenance through to its faulty functionality. The integrity of the original design and construction was sound. It still contained some warmth and value, but they were buried in a pile of eclectic collections gathered by an undiscerning landlord—me. My careless and undisciplined management resulted in deterioration, unwanted furnishings, and unexpected occupants. These distractions have almost always had unhappy effects. At times, they've even produced frightening consequences.

The Spirit is proving to possess the discernment and skills of a professional property manager, leading me to understand and renovate the house. Central to my learning curve is the Bible, or the Word of God as some call it. Previously I had no idea that this kind of information was in the Bible. Even though it was written more than two thousand years ago, in various languages, the pages I'm reading with the Holy Spirit's guidance right now prove to be dynamically relevant in addressing my present needs.

It contains truth, the integrity of which has been inspired and protected by God through hundreds of years of otherwise fallible human recording and translation. My encounter with the still-living Jesus the Christ has been astounding and logic-defying. However, I have no difficulty believing that this truth is intact and could remain intact and available to me today. Such a feat would be simple in comparison to what has been happening to me personally.

Until entering this experience, I both ignored and rejected the possibility of anything useful for today's world being contained in this book of antiquity. I intended to be the sole builder of my house, and certainly no one else's instructions were necessary. Needless to say, my project got off-track somewhere early in the process.

Most buildings erected without the benefit of proper engineering, materials, and supervision have crumbled and fallen. Mine was facing the same fate. Fortunately, I allowed Jesus, the carpenter from Galilee, to get past my protestations of pride and disbelief. He encouraged me to take a critical look at the house I was building—the intended temple of the Holy Spirit. Not only was it not comfortable to live in, it also could not provide protection from the storms that can come along from life.

Once I appraised my building honestly, it was easy to observe its desperate need for evictions, cleaning, repairs, renovations, and the implementation of a consistent and appropriate maintenance program. With the assistance of the new boarder, the Bible is proving to be a custom how-to manual for me, far exceeding the best home repair book in stores today.

I realize now Paul's words that initially caught me are not implying anything sinister. He is simply letting me know God has called to my attention that there is a better choice I can make. I can get off the destructive path I have been on and instead head towards a safe, healthy destination.

It's time for me to get back to work. What's next?

Room Key
experiencing forgiveness

1 CORINTHIANS 13:1–13

It's day thirty nine. The renovation continues with each day's reading and prayer. My wall of protective isolation, built by the stone and steel of my thoughts, is being removed and these verses explain how. Faith, hope, and love are the tools used to do the job.

Love came first—God's love for me. As I eventually recognized it and its authenticity, hope flickered and finally shone. This, in turn, encouraged me to think of those things that I did want in my life and engaged me in the plan to clean out bad habits, memories and attitudes .It is being done with God's Holy Spirit as guide, teacher and helper just as the Bible promised. With each small success, I am given the proof my ever-doubtful mind requires, deepening my belief in the Bible's truthfulness. Cracks are appearing in the wall I have been building since childhood as the Spirit patiently brings me to a level of trust where I have been able not only to unlock the cell door, but swing it wide open.

Once I opened it, the iron cell no longer restricted the movements of my special boarder. Until this victorious moment, I had invited the Spirit in but not really allowed free access to the entire space, intending to keep hidden the remaining dark junk. The boarder honoured the restrictive house rules, though the Spirit knows better than I what lurks in the unseen corners.

While embarrassing me with intrusion into those dark places is not the objective of the Spirit, helping me to unlock them and clean them out certainly is. My resistance makes the process unfold slowly, but thankfully it doesn't halt the progress. As I allow the Spirit to look into more hiding places, I discover that I am able to see more of myself.

These verses force me to think about my father and my experience of him when I was a child. While doing that, thoughts about his childhood come to me. Facts that I have known for a long time but never really considered come to mind.

His childhood was brought to an abrupt end at the age of 12 when his strict father committed suicide. As one of nine children, his widowed mother could no longer provide for them all so he and two siblings were shipped off to Canada. Once here, the siblings were separated and my father, as the youngest, got to stay with an aunt he did not know and work for her family as a farmhand. At twelve years of age!

Until this reading, I've never considered how harsh this childhood was for my father. Where did he receive or learn about a father's love? If he didn't know how to love, how could he love me or my mother? Yet I have blamed him and been bitter all my life so far because he didn't. Even at a very young age, the hurt I felt gradually distanced me from him and I unconsciously started to build the wall around my heart for protection. Somewhere along the line it became *my* rejection of him; *my* anger at him.

Ever since, I—and others—have constantly had to face the consequences of the resulting conflict.

The clarity of these thoughts startle me; I've never seen my problem this way before.

Many times, since starting this journey through the Bible, I have noticed how often there is reference to the "heart" of a person, the same awareness of myself that I have described in these notes. Today's words from the letter to the Corinthians has certainly unlocked my heart.

Jesus, through his Spirit, has shown me that, though it is necessary to greet him with the open-eyed wonder and trust of a child, it is just as vital for me to understand him with maturity and the willingness to shed my childish ignorance.

In my reading so far, I have learned forgiveness is available to any and every person who comes to God in prayer with a truly repentant heart. Jesus explains it is made possible by his death. I have experienced it—remembering again that night I read my list. I have learned forgiveness neither trivializes the wrong actions nor makes them right. Regardless of being the forgiver or the forgiven— forgiveness erases. This act eliminates the need to carry the weight of guilt and creates a desire to not reoffend. It makes it possible to truly live each day rather than just survive it.

The familiar words about forgiveness in the Lord's Prayer come to mind. I decide to stop feeling like I do not deserve to be forgiven and instead fully accept that promised forgiveness for myself, and in turn honestly give it to those I am angry at—starting with my father. After that, I better make things right with the people I have hurt.

The virtual key Jesus put in my pocket comes to mind. I think I know its name now—it is Forgiveness. It belongs in the Boarding House. I expect it will always be valuable, so I'll keep it handy, always ready to use.

Check the Spec Sheet
questioning again

PSALM 139

This psalm was written by David, a man who found the courage and took the time to examine himself using God's standards rather than his own and those of his peers.

Most of us know David was the young boy who won great fame through his slingshot victory over the giant, Goliath. He grew to be a man who was very faithful to God and consequently wrote many songs to express his thankfulness, preserved here in the book titled Psalms. The words he wrote are still quite valuable in teaching us today. They have the power to comfort us when we are troubled, or to express praise and thanks to God when our own words feel inadequate. Often David's phrases articulate my feelings better than I can myself.

In this psalm, he tells about the completeness of God's knowledge of each one of us, starting with our creation in the womb. Though there is very little in it that would satisfy a scientific inquiry, because of what I have learned this produces in me a feeling of safety and connectedness to God. It is a strange and wonderful sensation to read the thoughts of another person and feel as though they are your own. It's especially valuable to me because I know what a great and faithful man David was. Hopefully the similarity in our thoughts indicates that I'm on the right track.

Stretching back, I sit and soak in this peace of heart and mind. After a generous portion of time, the Spirit guides me towards a new insight.

David writes about the constant presence of God and never being able to escape it, he captures the powerful sense of safety that I have with God. No matter what the circumstance, no matter what temporary mood of mine would try to interfere, no matter what wrong deed I am guilty of, God is not going to leave me. This promise has been my lifeline. It has kept me from being washed away by whatever tide batters me.

My confidence in surviving both real and imagined dangers comes from knowing that God is aware of my every breath. My will to change myself to something better, my hope for protection, and my expectation that my existence is meaningful all find their source in this promised presence of God. I pray, pout, laugh, argue, cry, and learn as each day of my life is shared with this friend I describe as my boarder—the Holy Spirit. All of this is confirmed for me through the reading of this psalm. Yet I am also troubled by the words of love and assurance that David wrote. Why?

I am struck by the thought that I don't know Jesus in the same warm, loving way as I know God and the Spirit. I met him, of course, at that first "shove", on the porch, and again at the cell visit but I haven't had any physical or visual contact with him since that night when I answered the doorbell. Where is he? Why hasn't he allowed me to know him personally?

I know that God is described as a trinity, or one being with three distinct identities—the Father, the Son, and the Holy Spirit. It is difficult, if not impossible, to understand how one being is comprised of three. The closest I can come is by viewing myself from the perspective of other people. My children, for example, know me as "Dad" and my words and actions with them are very specific and unique. To the friends of my children, I am "Mr. Elliott." Again, my interactions with them are specific and unique. Friends and business acquaintances know me as "Greg," and once more there is an easily definable difference in how they relate to me. Yet there has to be a basic continuity in all of those perspectives, because I am only one person. It is a woefully inadequate model to describe God, but it has enabled me to at least hold an otherwise incomprehensible image of life and creativity.

I believe in and have met these three distinct realities of God. My belief at this point, though, is part of my problem. My relationship is so animated with the Two that I am troubled by the absence of the Third. In fact, I wonder whether perhaps Jesus does not approve of me and does not like me. I feel both anger and hurt in response to this assumption. How could this great guy we read about in the Bible, who accepted even the worst sinners in love and understanding, ignore me? What must I do to win his acceptance and love? I ask this question with a tone of complaint.

My question is answered with a long review of the relationships I've had with other people. This leads to a sharp, focused reminder of how much of my life has been spent in fits of anger, jealousy, self-pity, sarcasm, broken promises, and neglected relationships. I count the long hours and effort spent on my artwork at the expense of my marriage and children. I'm confronted by my deliberate dodging of the love offered to me by my mother and sisters. I wince at the realization of how my lack of insight into my father's hurts led me to reject a relationship with him. My selfish attitude, which has subjected my relationships with everyone and everything else to second place in my life, is painfully obvious.

I can see what a waste my arrogance and ignorance have made of the precious gift of life David writes about in Psalm 139. How will I ever be able to overcome all the damage I've done to other people and myself through intention and neglect?

The image of Jesus, as I briefly saw him that first time, appears like a freeze-frame. This time, I am able to closely observe his face. I had not done so during the scuffle that initiated this experience. Next, as a split screen, an image of Jesus appears in my mind as he stood behind the Spirit on the porch after ringing the doorbell. I had not taken the time to notice his expression then, either.

Now, as I study both of these images, I feel his eyes, full of love and caring, embrace me and see that he has had the same look in both of those encounters. I cry in a flood of shame and gratitude.

R.S.V.P.

answering the question

LUKE 2:1–20

My complaint about Christ's relationship with me is evidently going to continue to be addressed in this excerpt from Luke's writing. It is the story of the first Christmas. Most of us have heard it in one form or another, as churches call us to the "real reason for the season" and merchants call us to share the capacity of our credit cards.

Reading this story, my focus is drawn to the shepherds who were visited by the angels. Another virtual diorama forms and I picture myself standing with them on that hilltop overlooking Bethlehem. Slowly, gently, I am absorbed into the scene. There is no conversation between the shepherds, only the sounds of the sheep shuffling and bleating. I instinctively know that my role here is as a shepherd. I have an almost overwhelming awareness of responsibility to keep these sheep fed, watered, and safe. The air is chilly and, in the moonlit darkness, rocky drops and shadows promise danger, heightening the seriousness of the job. Without speaking to them, I know that the other shepherds are committed, no-nonsense people, strong and not easily thrown off by unexpected confrontations or threats.

The sensation of being there is very real and I am fully cognizant of every detail within the scene. The experience is like a lucid dream.

A brilliant flash of light takes my breath away. I see nothing else. It is only possible for me to know what took place in those moments through the words written by Luke in description of that night's events.

I am fully aware of the activity immediately following the angelic visit. This small group of shepherds is shaken by what has taken place. Their hardiness has been completely overturned. A period of animated discussion ensues before their accustomed pattern of rational matter-of-factness regains some slight measure of control over the situation. In sparing words, they speak to each other, trying to understand what has happened. I want to tell them what I know from having read the Bible some two thousand years into the future, but no explanation ventures forth from my lips.

Several agree to leave immediately for the tiny village, its lights visible down the hills from where we stand. Two have regained their composure and gruffly announce that they are not interested in going, choosing to remain with the flocks. The others start the downward trek, banding unusually close together as they depart.

I remain motionless and apart from them, the bursting activity of my mind imitating a fireworks display.

Those heading down the hill have just experienced something they will never forget or be able to adequately describe. When they get to the stable and baby, their thinking will be challenged in such an awesome manner as to change their lives forever. When they recount this story to their friends and neighbours, they will be rebuffed by incredulity. At this moment, they do not realize the impact that this baby will have on them and history, but I do. I can't believe that I'm here at the beginning. Nor can I believe what I'm about to do.

I know that the invitation to go to the child includes me, and I want to follow this little group of shepherds. However, my feet remain firmly planted to the patch of ground beneath me. Questions explode in my mind: What about my responsibilities here? Do I have to leave everything here to follow this baby who is God's son? What about my own family? Will this baby expect something from me? What about my plans?

I watch as the last of the small group slowly drops from sight over the ridge. I experience an intense desire to go with them and meet this baby, but I'm too afraid to leave my post. The two remaining shepherds have silently moved off to their customary stations.

The scene before me dissolves and is softly replaced with thoughts of three babies and their parents. The first baby is me, being held by my father and mother. Baby number two is my own firstborn as he lay on the bed with my wife, an hour after his birth. The third is Jesus with his parents Mary and Joseph, on the night of his birth. As gently as they came, the images leave.

I ask the Spirit for help in understanding this. I feel the warmth of the boarder's presence. I reread the verses, and this time they illuminate the thoughts of my heart like a flashlight in a darkened room. As the shaft of light moves through the darkness, I see the previously unrecognized connectedness lying there.

I recall my own childhood as the firstborn, and the aching I felt within me for softness and acceptance from my father. Throughout my childhood, he appeared to see only the successes of others and all of my failures. My mother tried to compensate, but that was not what I wanted. Except for brief hours here and there, his acceptance of me never came. Though I tried numerous times to earn his attention and affection, each attempt ultimately failed and left me feeling less willing to risk another.

The image of my own newborn son reminds me of my determination at the time to be a different and better father for my own children. Somehow the reality of my shortcomings interfered with my resolve and I didn't deliver on my promises to him, which eventually resulted in conflict between us. The ache returns. Now I am desperate for *his* love and acceptance.

Recently I complained to God about Jesus' aloofness, inferring that he didn't care for me, and in doing so I gave evidence of yet another relationship in which I was feeling a void—my relationship with Jesus. My response to the invitation those shepherds and I received on the hill was an RSVP card with the "Not attending" box checked.

Sitting in the company of my quiet friend, the boarder and site manager of this project, it is finally safe to admit how afraid I really am of again failing to measure up to a standard, and this time it is Jesus who is not about to accept me until I measure up. The standard my father required was never met, or at least it was never acknowledged. The fatherly standard I set for myself, as I observed it from great father/son relationships around me, has still not been met. Now I am faced with another standard to measure up to. Based on the previous standards, the likelihood of my succeeding with this one seems slim, and therein lies the source of my fear and lack of trust in myself. Unfortunately, I have tried to hide them by accusing Christ of failing to accept me.

The boarder continues the flashlight's slow dance across my mind. Formerly isolated thoughts begin to connect with each other. What must be obvious to others is now slowly becoming evident to me. There is a common thread running through the three stories of firstborns—my response to each of the individuals in these stories has been the same.

Through the Spirit's illumination, it becomes apparent that, at some point, I surrounded my emotions with a protective fence in response to my father. This fence was constructed and maintained by a negative attitude and stubborn pride. Unchecked, in time it became my operating personality. I lacked the ability to be compassionate and selective, keeping everyone at a distance and effectively holding me in. By the time the guy in the white shirt introduced himself to me, I had been feeling like a hostage.

Today, God's Spirit is giving me a follow-up lesson about jail cells. I received the first of these lessons in the early days of my reading and praying, while protesting my detention. Some of the bars of that cell were identified for me. At the time, I saw other bars I could not identify. It appears that their turn has come.

Remembering all this brings something else to mind that I had forgotten. Just as that first lesson drew to a close, I received a key. I knew it was the key to the cell's door—but I didn't use it. Obviously, it was the ultimate escape plan. As I find myself back in that same cell, I notice that the key is once again in my pocket, where I left it. What does it represent?

Now, two of my metaphors converge on each other—that of the fence, and that of the cell. As an unintentional result of the fence I built in response to childhood perceptions of my father, I am now my own jailer. The fence was built from the inside. The design was effective. As my life continued, I encountered other events and people who, in one way or another, disappointed or hurt me. It seemed logical to add another layer to the fence's height, to protect myself from further potential assaults. In time, it grew to an insurmountable height and became so tangled that it formed an impenetrable wall. The entrance was very small and, to further reduce the risk of intrusion, I remained inside the gate, never venturing out.

My unwillingness to be vulnerable with other people eventually rendered me unable to accept any goodness offered to me. At the same time, it robbed me of the capacity to extend goodness to anyone else. Though it was not my intention, I created the ultimate vulnerability—loneliness.

The fence/cell I built has no similarity to the temple described in the letters Paul wrote to the earliest church members. This dwelling place is certainly not a suitable home for God's Holy Spirit. Come to think of it, all indications are that it's not suitable for me, either.

So why didn't God just give me a kick on the backside and keep me from doing this? Such an intercession would have prevented a lot of discouragement and hurt. In fact, I see many other opportunities where God could simply inject new attitudes and behaviour and thus prevent a tremendous amount of upset and hurt from ever happening. Wouldn't that be better for all of us?

This question doesn't elicit any obvious response, which usually indicates that I need to re-examine the information already under my nose. Excepting the initial push/pull into this experience, I realize that every encounter I've had with God—either as the Creator, Jesus, or the Holy Spirit—has come in the form of an invitation which I am free to accept, decline, or reject entirely.

All those days when I decided my schedule was too busy to spend time with the Spirit; my answer today in the hillside invitation; those times when I had the opportunity to respond to someone using these new insights but didn't—on each of these occasions, it was demonstrated that my own will had primacy and the power to exert itself over God's will or hope for me, and I don't recall that there was even much of a struggle. This is a disturbing, frightening realization.

A mental light bulb clicks on as I remember that pivotal night when Christ rang the doorbell. Even in my wrongness and need, he would not take away my freedom of choice. Until I offered a genuine invitation, the Spirit would not coerce or impose entry to my heart and mind. I never lost my freedom to make my own choices, nor was my responsibility relieved. The presence of Christ and the Spirit on the porch tells me that my needs were known and that I was lovingly watched and protected through danger, but their interference with the follies of my choices was not possible without my permission. Either this plan was pure craziness, or it was born of the purest love.

I have been ensnared and in need of rescue for a long time, though it has taken me almost as long to realize that I am also the trapper. On that visit to the cell some time ago, that key Jesus left with me, represents a promise, signifying that release is in my own hands. No longer do I have to wallow in anger or self-pity, blaming my imprisonment on other people and events. Those excuses are no longer relevant. Jesus, who I accused of not caring for me enough to let me know him personally, visited and placed the escape key in my pocket. He really does care about me, in spite of my having snubbed him for so long. Is this what those highway signs mean when they garishly proclaim "Jesus Saves"?

"I died for you."

Who's There?
staring down lingering doubt

LUKE 1:26–38, PSALM 139, PSALM 23, PROVERBS 8

Today's session picks right up from yesterday. The Spirit apparently wants to make absolutely certain that I know beyond a shadow of a doubt whether or not Jesus accepts me.

The first of today's cluster of readings comes from Luke 1:26–38. It's the story of the young girl, Mary, who was to become the mother of Jesus. As in the case of the shepherds, the courier is once again an angel. Even this angel's name is provided—Gabriel—a personal touch that has a very positive effect on me. I never thought of them as having personal names.

It is easy for me to imagine Mary's state of mind. The appearance of such a being would be startling enough without the additional shock that she was to become pregnant even though she had never engaged in sexual activity and was already promised to be married. Can you imagine the impact this would have on her youthful dreams and hopes for the future? By accepting what God asked of her, Mary had to upset all the plans she'd excitedly made for her life. Her belief in God was starkly obvious. There was not one question from her, unlike a gaggle of my own, starting—just as Scrooge asked the first visiting spirit—with the question, "Are you real?"

Her faith and trust in God are equally easy to see. Realizing how dramatically affected her life was to be from that point on, without even being able to comprehend why God would ask such service from her, she nonetheless emphatically answered, "YES."

I look back sheepishly at my own response when simply invited to visit this baby on the eve of his birth. Questions immediately came forth, making apparent my mistrust of the situation. There was no humility at being so honoured, no pleasure at such a demonstration of God's reality—just selfish suspicion.

In Mary's story, God also sent the angel to prepare Joseph, her husband-to-be, for his role in this event. Understanding the social scandal he would surely face as a result of these circumstances, Joseph nonetheless accepted this incredibly demanding request God placed on him. What a difference there is between Joseph's answer and mine! He must have had fear and doubt in his heart and mind, but he didn't stand there protesting. Instead, he demonstrated his trust in God.

Why am I so afraid of answering God?

I think of my questions posed on the hillside while watching the shepherds set out to meet the baby in a manger. Those queries thinly masked my greatest fear, that of being separated from my wife, children, and friends.

It's a reasonable fear. As the changes in my life progress, I see that my wife does not want to see or know Jesus in the way I do. Will a choice be necessary one day? The thought of this relationship with Jesus separating me from her strikes cold terror into my heart. Maybe if I stay back a bit and out of sight, it won't be necessary to choose between her and Jesus.

I desperately want to follow this man Jesus and see what he has to show me, but I can't possibly leave my wife behind. Why would God bring this woman into my life and then ask me to choose between him and her? Maybe that's not what's really happening, but I don't want to take the risk. I have allowed myself to expect that Jesus could exert his power on me to obtain the response he wants. I am not willing to be controlled, and as tough as I think I am, I know I am no match for God if it comes to a fight.

Did Joseph have this same fear of God but keep it hidden? Did Mary? They lived in a small rural community which had strict standards. Pregnancies out of wedlock fell short of those standards. Everyone would know about it through the gossip lines. They faced major changes in their lives along with humiliation and criticism from families and neighbours. Were they simply more afraid of God than of the social price they would pay? Their words don't seem to indicate that. What, then, is so different about me? How can I still think this way after all I have been shown?

My Do-It-Yourself cell is doing its job.

The project manager nudges me and I remember the key.

David's words in Psalm 139 remind me again of the impossibility of hiding from God. They also remind me of how much love God has given to my creation and life so far. In spite of the cell of spiritual seclusion I have successfully constructed, God knows exactly where I am and can articulate my needs better than I.

David's words let me see that he, too, was in a frame of mind in which he felt powerless. He needed something beyond his inadequate intellect. His words mirror my own desperation and frenetic search for answers. He, too, shows the disappointment with himself that I am feeling. David ended his psalm with a request for God to examine and test him. He obviously trusted God and expected to be led safely through whatever answers the examination produced.

If a man of David's stature was willing to submit himself and the anguish in his mind to such an act of faith, there is no reason for me to fear doing the same. These calls to follow have perhaps served as a test for me. An exam's purpose is usually to reveal to the examiner what the examined individual knows, but in this case I think God wanted *me* to see what is in my heart.

The Spirit's nudge transforms into a big hug with this thought, confirming that I am on the right track. The words and images from Psalm 23 now follow and assist me in envisioning the security and protection which surround me always, whether I'm aware of it or not. The shepherd David describes here could only love and serve, never force or manipulate.

Almost like a reward for the breakthrough I have finally made, Proverbs 8 ends this session by describing the rich benefits of wisdom. These verses bring all the earlier thoughts together and sew the pieces into a quilt of understanding. Though there is still fear in me, I now feel the warmth of confidence to challenge it. I do not need to fear, especially not Jesus.

It is time to unlock the cell door and prop it open—maybe even hang a flowerpot and a Welcome sign beside it.

Shipping Label
direct delivery, belonging

LUKE 24:46–49

L ike a spoiled child, my hectic daily schedule continues to demand priority and if I yield to it my prayer time gets bumped and I am launched without connecting to this source of my life energy and direction. This is far too valuable to me now so I am determined to make those precious moments available first thing every day. Today I walked to the office, inviting the Spirit to join me, free from interruptions, emails and voicemail summonses, releasing God from call waiting.

Swishing through the yellow leaves of autumn today, I could smell the warmth of the sun and hear the quiet calm of the neighbourhood. Everything seemed to be right and affixed to its purpose. Time seemed suspended. All the concerns and demands of the business world were silenced.

While passing through the golden hue of the trees and shrubs, I got a sense of my own transparency. Rather than feeling like an observer or intruder of this peaceful harmony of sight and sound, I experienced the surrealistic sensation of being a part of it.

For a few precious moments, I was able to know fully that I am an integral part of the same creation that holds together the sun, trees, and calm air. I am a forgiven person and therefore belong in this tableau of innocence. This walk in the sunshine allowed me to feel completely free of the weight of past stupid things I have done. Today's prayer walk unequivocally tells me that I am officially free of any such load, regardless of my harsh self-judgment.

This weightless awareness has me elevated as I return and begin this day's reading. The words come from Luke's account of Jesus' last couple of hours on earth following his resurrection. Not long ago, I would have said that such an absurd claim belonged only on the cover of a grocery store gossip tabloid. But that was then, and this is now. No single reading or moment convinced me of Christ's continuum of life, yet my doubt slowly reshaped itself into hope that it was true, and from hope to belief. I still cannot explain how Jesus could come back to life, but because of what I have experienced and read in the Bible, I unquestionably believe he did.

Unlike the disciples in Jesus' day, I have not seen Jesus in the flesh. But like them, I know he is alive.

Incidents like this morning's walk enable me to see and learn what God is showing me through the lives of the people in the Bible. It is always about love. It is not a contractual love as between lovers, or a self-fulfilling love as found in popular music or literature, or a possessive love demonstrated in a collection of sports cards or old license plates. Neither is it the fantasy love portrayed in a movie or romance novel. It's not even the worrisome or fawning love of a parent. It is more than any of these.

God's love is free of all conditions and frivolities, giving dimension and wholeness to whoever accepts it. Included with his love is the possibility of exemption from penalty for those who have done wrong or chosen to do nothing when faced with the opportunity to do something good.

Is this important? How do we know what is "wrong"? I think of my earlier observation of the jail cell of thought and attitude that imprisoned me. It was rendered like an editorial cartoon, in which the bars were named and labelled to ensure that I understood their significance. The lack of forgiveness in my life, both given and received, accounted for a significant number of those bars.

Long before psychiatry was able to offer explanations of why and how our personal moral values can affect our lives, Bible stories identified their potential advantages and dangers. The world is God's creation and it is formed using laws and principles that, like science, must be understood and followed if we are to avoid problems. Through the use of words like "conscience," we acknowledge that we have an intuitive ability to know when we have done something wrong. Unfortunately, many of us choose to ignore this spiritual voice, or fail to give it much more than a derisive acknowledgement. Each generation lists, categorizes, and ranks "wrongdoing." Laws are written to define and address our transgressions. We argue the fine points of what constitutes good or bad morality and behaviour. Examples of sin, as defined by God, are displayed in the Bible along with Jesus' teachings to prepare us for the complications and consequences of ignoring these warnings.

How much can our contrary behaviour affect us? Who will know if I think wrong thoughts? What does it matter if I do something wrong, as long as I don't get caught? An answer appears in the two statements Jesus frequently made before performing a miraculous healing. He would either cite the person's faith as the key to their healing or say that their sins were forgiven, after which the healing would be apparent. The statement about forgiveness indicates that sin was either the source of their trouble or an obstacle to their healing and moving on in life. Once the person knew there was no need for them to be weighed down with shame or guilt, a new condition of thought and attitude opened the way for restoration of the body and mind. Their lives would be positively affected from that moment onward.

Is there any other reason given to recognize and admit those thoughts and actions that are contrary to God's law and hope for us?

Apart from the fact that contemporary medical science has verified that the guilt which follows sin can interfere with our mental and physical health, there are oft-repeated warnings throughout the Bible that the eventual penalty of sin is death.

This seems harsh to me and incongruent with the nature of God that I have experienced. Why talk about all this love and then threaten death? It must be vitally important to avoid breaking God's laws for the deterrent to be so powerfully presented. This frightens me, because I realize that I am already guilty of so many violations. Even since meeting Jesus and hearing this warning, I am bewildered by the ease with which I am still able to be a repeat offender.

By this absolute definition, I am guilty. It would mean there is no chance for me to escape the inevitability of paying the penalty—death. Given this, the rest of my days will be choked by a black cloud of reckless abandonment and despair. If death is the ultimate end, and I have already qualified for the penalty, why bother to change? Everyone dies anyway, whether he or she was good, bad, or somewhere in between.

Jesus, however, knows that physical death is not the absolute end. There is more, and his seemingly unrealistic love for us compels him to want to remove this fear of punishment for failure and rebellion. The death sentence is demanded by some universal balance of justice that I am yet unable to understand. Though it cannot be changed, Jesus does not want us to have to pay this penalty—yet he knows we will not be able to avoid it. So he did what every parent or sibling in a life or death situation would do for a loved one —he said, "Take me, and spare them." And that is what happened.

Everything he did or said occurred with the full knowledge that he was going to face the reality of a terrifying death, fully aware of each moment of the humiliating and painful process, knowing he was innocent of the vehement accusations made against him. He accepted this action as a class settlement to prepay the automatic death penalty earned by all those who break the universal laws of creation. Through this, since the penalty has already been paid, every lawbreaker is now given the option of accepting forgiveness and a fresh opportunity to live within the law. Now each of us has a choice between two options, each with its own terms.

The Bible reading I am doing indicates Christ desperately wants everyone to understand that we are both physical and spiritual beings. Our spiritual lives continue on the other side of physical death. How we live here prepares us for that future life and will dramatically impact its quality and direction when the day comes for us to go to it. This reminds me of the times I have gone through a customs gate in an airport and how the answers on my form determine which line I will be sent to next, and whether or not I will be subjected to a difficult process.

Jesus experienced everything in life I will ever have to face. He did not avoid sorrow, anger, temptation, rejection, and death because of who he is. Instead he took them on and demonstrated how to live with integrity through each of them as an example of how we can conquer them as well.

His reappearance after execution gave his disciples final proof of the existence of life after death, which human logic declares is not possible. I have personally discovered that he is still willing to provide that proof whenever he is earnestly asked for it. Many women, men, and children have, like the disciples, witnessed this incredible truth about the continued life of Jesus and his concern for us. History records his death, and through our understanding of mortality we know everyone dies physically at some point. So if a person has the opportunity to meet him interactively, it is incontrovertible proof, to that person at least, that he is alive and that there really is some other form of life after death, just as he said.

Knowing that he is alive is the lynchpin to understanding and believing who he is and what he taught. Yet even with this undeniable evidence, my own shallowness, impeded further by the jealous pawns of the dark principality of evil, often diverts me from accepting what Jesus freely offers. It is always my choice, which is both the wonder and the danger. I don't always choose correctly.

The dimension that Jesus presents cannot be measured or contained by formulae produced by our human sciences. It must be held in faith—knowledge that refuses to be substantiated by our recognized standards of evidence.

Unlike the love Christ gives to us without condition, this forgiveness does have a couple of conditions. First, it is necessary to believe the message. Second, it is essential to fully recognize our breaches of God's laws of love and admit them to God, honestly desiring to be redeemed.

I want this but I'm a bit reluctant to accept it because of embarrassment with my continued screw-ups in the face of the price Jesus paid so I could be free. My embarrassment makes me reluctant to approach God through prayer, confessing yet another wrongdoing. He must be as impatient with my constant stumbling as I am.

The Bible is telling me Jesus has already sent out the gift of forgiveness with the Holy Spirit. My walk this morning showed me the package with my name on the shipping label.

All I have to do is accept it.

A Winner!
recognizing and celebrating the changes

2 Timothy 1:6–14

Today's passage lands like a slap to the face. Paul's letter to his young assistant Timothy reminds him to keep alive the gift of the Holy Spirit. Keep alive?

From the little I've learned, it's clear that the Spirit cannot actually die, so I expect it's to remind us that it is possible to ignore or hesitate to accept the Spirit's presence. This gentle yet powerful Spirit offered but did not insist on entering a relationship with me. It was my choice to accept or reject. Any friendship requires the investment of *both* parties if it is to exist and develop. Extending trust to the other person is a necessary risk. Each party must fully participate through phone calls, visits, help with a project, or sharing celebrations and trials if the relationship is to grow. Paul's words indicate that I have to do my part to nurture this relationship if I want it to continue.

Thus far, I've primarily thought of the changes I'm experiencing as gifts. I interpret Paul's teaching however, to say that the Holy Spirit, and *relationship* with the Holy Spirit, is the real gift. As precious as any one gift of change is to my life, the value of a daily relationship with the *giver* of the gift is far greater. My view of this falls short of what Paul is saying.

During the past few weeks, I have felt radically different than during any other period in my life. In the past several days, since experiencing forgiveness, I have enjoyed an especially deep sense of calm within my thought life. I want it to last forever. What a gift that is to a mind that was always agitated, never slowing down or turning off! Resulting from that is a significant change in my behaviour. I now use the pocket-sized New Testament that I carry with me each day, reading a few verses whenever there's an interlude in my schedule. It gives me a quick boost, like having an energy bar in my pocket all the time. My days are now enjoyable.

I've felt inner calmness and an eagerness to read about God. These things alone are incredible, but there is more—I now believe in God's current presence in the world, and in my own life. This belief has given me a whole new awareness of my behaviour. I feel worthwhile and loved and want to love in return. Not only am I now becoming concerned about other people and how my behaviour will affect them, I want to behave in a manner that will find approval with my companion, the Spirit, who is aware of my every thought and deed. It all combines to provide wholeness. What a gift! It is not the invasive disciplinary control I first imagined it might be. My boarder infuses me with a sense of belonging to God and I want to be appropriately clean in my every thought and action.

No longer does it seem necessary to get impatient or angry with people or situations that are not going my way. It's like I've been released from steel manacles! I now look closer at the reality of my future life, which goes beyond my eventual physical death. The Spirit hints at my need to prepare for it. I never before believed that there's anything after death, figuring that once I am wearing my pine suit and planted in the ground, the game was over. To believe there is more has deeply enriched me with a reason to live today. Again, what a gift!

My resolve to receive the full measure of this internal newness grows daily. Even my patterns of speech have taken on new lightness. Until recently, the heaviness of my thoughts was evidenced in my words. Now hope can be heard. Another incredible gift!

The clamour of the Boarding House has been dramatically reduced, there is lightness in the atmosphere, and gentle laughter now skips out of many of its rooms.

These verses in the second letter to Timothy go further and help me begin to understand that there is more involved in my better state of mind than calmness, comfort, and freedom. These are merely evidences of the Spirit's presence, not its purpose. They are not the gift from God that Paul talks about in his letter. The gift is the Spirit, and the purpose of the Spirit is to enable us to have a full, life-enriching relationship with God through Jesus.

As I absorb this, I realize that these verses bring with them an expectation. Like an alarm clock signalling a new morning, they announce that it is time for me to get up and get going. It makes me realize that I'm not yet utilizing these new capabilities to any great extent outside of my own life.

Many of the verses I've read, today's included, indicate that the need for more active involvement is approaching. The trouble is, I'm hit by a disconcerting thought upon reading the words, *"Be ready to suffer with me"* (2 Timothy 1:8). This does little to encourage me to participate. I've had enough upset and struggle. Good thing that the previous verse assures me that God gives us the strength to do it.

Thus far, the noticeable changes in me have included calm, order, introspection, love, and learning. These are all major alterations. It is difficult to believe how all these things have taken place due to a person I cannot physically see or touch. It defies every particle of logic I am able to summon. But in this passage, Paul admonishes me to look at the other facets of the Spirit's personality within me.

Previous to this whole experience there had always been an odd sensation of a hole or emptiness that I was aware of, as if something was missing from me. Lately it feels like that space is being filled in.

Paul's words here indicate I should tell other people about the rearrangement that is taking place within me. I haven't done that yet. First, because I'm not sure how to describe it, and second, because I'm a bit afraid to do so. Will anyone understand, even if I can find adequate words? What will their responses be? Will they believe me?

However, beyond these reasons lies another, more significant one. Most of my life saw me quick to render sharp derision on anyone who professed to be "Christian." I would challenge and berate them. I didn't accord them respect, even in a miserly portion.

I obviously didn't understand what was involved in being a Christian. It made no sense to me why anyone would subject himself or herself to such a foolish belief. In fact, I often went to great lengths to dump my opinion on others and encourage them to see the "real" light, that of logic and common sense.

Is that the kind of person Paul is encouraging Timothy to be undaunted by?

Those people whom I attacked with my ignorant conviction must have known then what I am now discovering. My verbal abuse on their intellectual and emotional strength must certainly have caused them suffering. I have been one of those attackers, just like those people in the Bible who persecuted those early church builders. Like Paul, as people who knew and experienced God's love, they probably would have held for me the love and compassion I am now just starting to learn about.

A powerful sense of unworthiness floods over me. I have, in fact, done many things to disqualify me! Yet here I am.

I am reminded here that Paul also thought and felt this way and that I must not let that become a barrier between God and myself. I too can live a new life.

Though it is not found through a lottery ticket like those television commercials portray, I'm living the dream.

Knock, Knock
awareness beyond self

ROMANS 10:8–17, EPHESIANS 4:1–6

Lately I have been enjoying some of the benefits and seeing some of the possibilities of this changing life. Many of the worries and hang-ups I have developed over my years of separation from God are now gone. I have given up a lot of the guilt I carried around, which kept me feeling unworthy of relationships with decent people and, I suspect, kept them from approaching me. These are tenants that cause disruption in the house. I've been reaching out a bit and cautiously engaging with people in a new way. I haven't trusted myself to do this for a very long time. My freedom is real. Though I still experience shyness, my encounters with other people and situations are exhilarating. My keen awareness of the Spirit's company, and therefore the nearness of God, truly extends everywhere I go, dispelling my fear that his immediacy may exist only when I am sitting in the armchair reading the Bible.

I take walks in the neighbourhood and pay attention to the day-to-day life around me. I now feel completely fresh as I come into contact with people, seeing and hearing all that I've been missing out on. Nothing ever seemed happy or safe before I began this relationship with God. My eyes only managed to see the chaos in everything while my ears heard only the clamour of conflict. Even at this stage of the renovation, I am starting to view myself and everything around me positively. An attitude of hope is taking form in me, assuring me that I can change and better things are coming. This hope is directly rooted in what I am learning through reading the Bible and praying.

Today's passage heightens my awareness of my own actions. I want to do or say only those things that will bring a smile to God's face and change all those things about me that do not. I'm also finding balance within me, and because of it I no longer feel defeated by each new awareness of something I haven't done right. Instead I feel a strong motivation to overcome the obstacles that sharpen my spirit. I am determined to continue making progress. I feel more solid and intact than I have ever felt before.

Images come to me from some of those early readings, in which the work of building a temple for God's Spirit was described. I know that some very real and lasting construction has taken place in me. Though my own logic still wants to ask questions about why this has happened, the intuitive part of me, now receptive to the Spirit, assures me that the reason is not my uniqueness but the uniqueness of the truth in Paul's teaching.

While the construction is not complete—indeed, I am not yet a temple—I sense that I have progressed enough to begin my new life and function. So what's next? I find a complete and satisfying answer to this in chapter 10 of Romans .

I am a different person from the man who was trapped in the Mad Parade. At that time, I reached a state of extreme demoralization, not through intention but as a result of my stubborn attitude. My resistance had to be answered before I was willing to allow Jesus an opportunity to prove not only his existence but also his sacrificial love for me.

I was a slow learner, but this did not upset the work of the ever-patient Spirit. Like the lone grateful man from the group in the story of the ten lepers (Luke 17: 11-19), I want to give my thanks.

Until today's reading, I have not been sure how to formulate a response for the unbelievable change that has occurred. How can I express my gratitude? I look for the first time, in a caring way, at people around me—maybe there others like me who are struggling with their life because they don't know there is a way to fix it.

Maybe one day I will be able to knock on the door of another boarding house that has many locks and shuttered windows and tell them they don't have to live that way anymore.

The Neighbours
care for others

1 Corinthians 3:16–23

These verses and the thought I came to yesterday raise a point for me that should have been obvious. I know God's Spirit lives in me and there are lots more people around me. Are they like boarding houses as well?

Earlier in my introduction to the Bible, I was both humoured and puzzled by the verses that claimed it was God's desire for each person to become a temple where the Holy Spirit could dwell. The very real unfolding of that improbable-sounding transformation has been the basis of my reconstruction from an angry, fearful, tense person to one developing a positive, expectant faith in God.

Gaining a better understanding of my complicated psychological, physiological, and spiritual structure and discovering the reality of God's existence has given me excitement and hope, both for myself and the people in the world around me. It has dramatically reduced my untrusting resistance to anything outside of my own logic, and opened me to a loving partnership of protection and guidance. Each day is a discovery of hidden treasure. Within me is the wonderful sense of excitement one observes in the old tradition of a child opening the doors and windows of a Christmas Advent calendar, anticipating and yet surprised each time by the chocolate treat contained within.

As I grow more comfortable with the new me, I take notice of the lives of other people around me. Are they experiencing the same thing?

Greg R. Elliott

Thinking of other people as a virtual house like me would form a neighbourhood. Each house in the neighbourhood containing its own life and stories, just as my Boarding House does in representing me. Right from the beginning of my encounter with Jesus, I knew there was nothing I had done to deserve this incredible meeting. I quickly learned from my unsophisticated prayers and secluded Bible reading that my long list of wrong-doing does not disqualify me from having a relationship with God. What I am experiencing is available to anyone who asks.

The neighbourhood includes people I see or know about, whether close by or elsewhere in the world. This metaphor helps me see the connectedness and mutual responsibilities that neighbours have for one another. You are one of my neighbours and I am one of yours.

Though acknowledging the near impossibility of complete accuracy, we all know it is possible to form quick assessments of each other based on what we see and hear, directly or indirectly. Sometimes rules or circumstances restrict our relationships with each other, but primarily we each choose how we will involve ourselves with the other people who share the world with us. All of us can provide a reason for our particular choice. But what is the basis of our decision?

I guess who we perceive ourselves to be will determine who we think our neighbours are and how we involve ourselves in life.

In the course of this unexpected series of encounters with God, I have made the surprising discovery that I am not the person I thought I was, nor am I as alone in the crowd as I believed. My neighbours don't always prove to be who I think they are, either.

Most of my perception of the world comes through the accepted channels of formal education, media reporting and advertising. The knowledge disseminated there has many sources—both reliable and otherwise. All society holds much of this information in common, and as such it becomes the benchmark of credibility from which we judge all things.

A commonly accepted view holds that science is the source of all we are and all that exists around us. Through science we can know all and do all, once we discover the equations that give us control over producing particular results. This attitude, if applied with integrity and good will, is extremely creative and has served the human race well as we strive to survive and progress.

I viewed myself and other people through this scientific standard, but eventually recognized that there simply had to be something more. The source of life had to run deeper than a few complicated biological formulae. My still-

136

unfolding relationship with the unseen person of the Holy Spirit is proving that there is, indeed, much more.

As I have allowed myself to be pried open by the wisdom contained in the Bible, my definition of science has changed. Now I am able to see it as the act of discovering the ingredients and methodology God uses in creating us and the world, and the universal laws that sustain both. God is the creator while science is his toolbox of creation. Our talents at probing and harnessing science are among the specific gifts God has equipped us with, to exercise and express the creative free will that is part and parcel of creation. How we have used and misused these gifts fills the volumes of history.

This leads me to believe that people who view science as our source will celebrate great accomplishments, while those who recognize science as the explanation of God's work will accomplish and enjoy far more.

The Bible's teachings have significantly expanded the conventional knowledge I previously held. Instead of the further contradictions I sceptically expected to find in the Bible, I have found the connectedness that was missing from my life.

How does all this fit into the metaphor of the neighbourhood? By understanding who I am to God, I am able to appreciate how each person around me is also loved and valued. They are all in some stage of development—where I was, where I am now, or where I may one day be in my relationship with God. This fresh perspective creates in me an awareness of other people as spiritual siblings rather than competitors. God not only wants me to know this for my own benefit but also to enact it with other people and encourage them.

The necessity and benefit of understanding this relationship is practically and powerfully demonstrated in the teaching and healing work of the disciples, past and present. Paul, who wrote so much of the New Testament, was so exceptional in his grasp of what God showed him that his recorded thoughts are still able to reach deep within me and unlock new potential. In terms of the metaphor, you could say he was an early proponent of the neighbourhood renewal projects we read about so often today.

I'm starting to feel a bit that way myself.

Prior to that first "shoving" encounter with Jesus, I avoided contact or friendship with other people. Yes, there were a few that tolerated me but for the most part I was too abrasive and self-focused to want to reach out to other people. I really didn't care about them.

That attitude is changing in me. I'm starting to look at other people and wonder how they are doing in their inner lives. I am concerned for the ones who appear to be struggling like I was. Now instead of seeing them as unlikable or combative as I once did, I am hoping they can find what I am discovering.

Writing this brings a chuckle to my mind as I picture the boxes of stuff and the tenants that were rounded up to start the Boarding House clean out. One of the rowdy tenants, named "Who Cares", has now moved out.

This place is certainly improving!

Neighbourhood Renewal
available to everyone

JOHN 21:1–19

The Bible makes it clear that death, the one thing almost all of us fear in life, has been conquered by Jesus. In this reading from John's record, shortly after the crucifixion, Jesus appears before some of his disciples, presumably to prove that he is alive.

Though unexplained, his physical appearance is somehow different and the disciples do not immediately recognize him. Since his death, they have returned to their trade, and at this moment they are returning from having spent the entire night fishing. Their net is empty, but in response to a few words of direction from Jesus, their years of experience seem to count for little as they dip the net once more and it returns to the surface straining to contain its catch.

This miracle was not intended to belittle their knowledge or effort, but rather to demonstrate once again Jesus' reality and authority. He easily changes the conditions that all of their combined skills, knowledge, and logic were unable to effect. This incident demonstrates that we may take for granted his willingness and desire not only to provide us with our needs, but also to go beyond even, to abundance.

By the time the disciples join him on the shore, they realize who he is. After serving the breakfast he has prepared for them, Jesus engages in an interesting Q and A session with Simon Peter. Three times Simon is asked whether he loves Jesus, and three times Simon replies that he does and that Jesus already knows it to be so. With each of Simon's answers, Jesus responds by telling him to take care of his sheep. It amuses me to picture a fisherman being given the job of tending someone's flock of sheep.

Simon's third response shows that being asked the question so many times annoys him. It is obvious that Jesus wants Simon to focus more closely on the question and the implications of his answer. Jesus uses an analogy to explain to Simon that his love for him will now carry new implications and that he will soon face demands to make decisions he would prefer to avoid.

Jesus is teaching his disciples. He is pushing them to fully understand both his love for them and how their love for him will need to be expressed. These disciples will have the responsibility of teaching others, so they themselves must understand Jesus and their relationship with him as fully as possible. The disciples, and men and women like them through the centuries, kept the message intact and passed it forward to us.

According to John 21, Simon's third affirmation of his love was given with a heavy heart. No doubt, Simon was feeling that Jesus didn't believe his proclamation of love or perhaps he felt he did not measure up to Jesus' expectations of him. I am well-acquainted with that feeling.

My perspective allows me to analyze the scene without getting personally involved. Simon obviously thinks it is enough to enjoy Jesus' love and return it to him. I can see Jesus' intent and I'm able to recognize the parallel between Simon and me. It is easier for me to see that Jesus, in his firmness, was not treating Simon with indifference or disbelief; he was teaching him to stretch past the comfort level that would produce satisfaction with only the obvious and instead view his assignment in its fullest. By doing this, Simon and all those he taught would receive everything Jesus came to give.

Jesus' odd directive to care for his sheep, in response to Simon's declaration of love, gives clear evidence that there is more to our relationship with Jesus than simply enjoying a private treasure. Jesus wants Simon—and I think all of us—to understand that his love is to be absorbed and then passed forward. It is a love with far more capacity and capability than simply serving the needs of a select few and making them feel good. Only days before this conversation on the beach, Jesus had been executed in a painful, humiliating, and unjustified assault. He claimed that this had to happen because he loved us, and because his intercession had life and death implications for our future. Now he stood beside the water with his students to ensure that they understood the awesome truth and reality of what he had taught them and done for us—his flock of sheep.

Until now, I have been concentrating on getting my own vacuum filled, having my own hurts healed and my own darkness illuminated. My acute need almost allowed me to settle for a much too shallow understanding of what Jesus was doing in this scene. I didn't see any reason to do anything with this but enjoy it. It is clear that Simon and I are not just to keep it to ourselves or simply return this love to the giver. We have been given something so big and so valuable that we can and should share it with many others.

It's not just all about me!

Happy Dance
expressing thanks

PSALM 111, LUKE 17:11–19

Today's readings express and capture my feeling of excitement and the electric awareness of opportunity as each day begins. I am interested in everyone and everything. I am happy to be alive. I have an unquenchable thirst to discover everything I can about God. The all-over sense of thankfulness I have been saturated with feels as though it is now a permanent state of being. All those bright, individual, life-giving moments I receive everyday from the Bible are coming together and shaping a new person—even though the guy in the mirror still looks like me.

The writer of Psalm 111 confirms that she or he, too, is aware of the incredible delight God brings into a person's life, once again articulating and confirming my own thoughts and feelings far better than I am able to do.

The characteristics described here, which have such a positive effect on me, are honour, patience, reverence, and praise. At one time, these words were barriers, preventing me from approaching God. I interpreted them as implying subjection and blind obedience. I had no desire to be amongst a mass of robots kneeling before some sci-fi deity. I still don't want to play such a role. Fortunately, I have learned that God does not want that either, from me or anyone else.

In today's second passage, Luke tells the story of ten men who suffered from leprosy, a terrible disease that not only struck at their physical health but also sentenced them to social isolation. They asked for and received healing from

Jesus, and I can only guess at the jubilation they must have experienced as they raced to rejoin their families and friends. It's easy to picture them dancing and flexing their restored bodies. I can imagine their frame of mind as they realized the potential of this healing and how it would change their lives. It must have produced an internal music that simply demanded a joyous response. I hear it, too.

Their path was different than mine though. Unlike me, they *asked* Jesus to heal them. Luke doesn't provide enough information to determine whether they did so out of a belief in God or because they heard the stories in the marketplace about Jesus' capabilities. Whenever there is an obvious lack of detail in the Bible, I have come to the conclusion it is either unimportant or deliberately omitted to provide room for more thought and examination on the reader's part. This has always resulted in greater insight for me.

Looking at these ten men's responses through my own experience, I think that only one of them came close to understanding the true source of his new health. The other nine may one day have examined it further, but not on this day. I'm not sure what happened in their lives, though it is easy for me to see that I was once like them—seize the moment.

Luke records Jesus' obvious disappointment in their lack of understanding and gratitude. However, there was no reneging on the healing. God promises that all who ask in faith will receive; they believed Jesus could heal them and so they received. There are no sticky conditions of propriety and form. I'm glad for that.

The prayers and Bible reading I do with the Spirit open up in me a whole new dimension of thought and awareness. I still examine this realm with a doubtful, often critical mindset that challenges every claim, hoping that Jesus realizes it is not my usual, stubborn arrogance still at work. My challenges are always welcomed and answered.

The answers are packaged in many forms and keep me alert. Often they come directly as an intellectual, thought-based product. Some come in the metaphoric dioramas I try to recapture and record. Many come through otherwise ordinary circumstances and events in my life. Encounters with people I know, and sometimes even complete strangers, are frequently used in a chain of amazing "coincidences" which confirm over and over the immediate truth and presence of God in my daily routine.

My sceptical inquiries are given logical, practical answers that I can understand. As the facts and experiences meld together over time, I become aware of how the process brings me to understanding. This process, in turn, helps me to become more receptive, producing calmness in me that allows greater discrimination and recognition of the Holy Spirit. I am thankful beyond expression for what I have learned and received. Like the one man in Luke's story who did understand, I have to find the words or actions to say "Thank you."

Though the reasons are different, my feeling of exclusion from mainstream society is equal to this man's. My self-evaluation has probably been as low as his and I can't imagine how his joy and enthusiasm could be any less than mine. Indeed, God delivered to both of us the full measure of the promise of love, provision, forgiveness and restoration made long before either of us was born. The same promise filled the writer of Psalm 111 with so much energy that he or she was inspired to create this song of praise.

No doubt a situation would in time come into the life of the healed man when the realities and evil of this world tried to defeat him again. There might even have been many such times, but he would surely always have this moment of promise, a moment in which he met the author of his victory, to turn his scramble for existence into another dance of celebration. The unnamed psalm writer and Luke, each writing centuries apart from each other, deliver the same message of promise for anyone who will receive it. Today, I am living it and dancing it.

Multilingual
confidence and affirmation

ACTS 2:1–36

In this reading, which takes place shortly after Jesus' death, the disciples experience the first effect of having the Holy Spirit with them. The disciples, all Galileans, have just preached about Jesus to a large group of people, many who are travellers from other countries. The amazing occurrence here is that these visitors were able to understand the disciples as if they had been spoken to in their native languages—and considering their different places of origins, they obviously spoke a wide assortment of languages and dialects.

Many religious leaders from various regions were included in this crowd, gathered presumably in response to the event of Jesus' crucifixion and the accounts of his disciples living at this particular location. Peter, one of the better known disciples, addressed the entire crowd, explaining that the disciples were neither linguists nor rambling fools affected by alcohol. This ability to communicate universally was a gift of God's Holy Spirit and further proof of what the Scriptures and prophecies claimed.

I am both surprised and relieved by the fact that Peter is speaking. This is a man whose personality and behaviour have impressed me so far in my reading of the Bible. I have formed a clear, positive image of him based on the accounts of his words and actions since Jesus recruited him. Prior to that turning point, he had been a partner in a successful fishing business, which leads me to assume that he was both physically fit and mentally astute. Hard work was probably more a delight than a necessity for this man. He boldly spoke his mind and often challenged the statements Jesus made for further explanation. He possessed all the idealized attributes of masculinity and strength of character any man could wish for—he was a "man's man" in other words—and yet unashamedly admitted his dependence on God. I respect and like this man, his name is on my short list of men and women whose lives exemplified the qualities of faith and personality I want to achieve. I wanted to see myself in him.

However, I was extremely disturbed by Peter's fearful denial of any affiliation with Jesus—not just once, but three times (Luke 22:55–60) during the night after the arrest of Jesus. The depth of my disappointment in him was indicative of the lack of courage I felt within myself. If Peter, this man of great strength whom I admired so much, couldn't face such a fear, how could I ever expect to?

Today, however, I once again see the promise for me as Peter speaks to that crowd, unintimidated by their academic stature or any legal or social threats they pose. He is filled with the truth Jesus taught and with courage from the Holy Spirit.

Fortunately, I haven't been called to such a public podium as Peter, but through him I have been encouraged not to hide in a corner of shame and fear. So far, there has not been any need for me to speak in a foreign language as those disciples did, though I have been given the opportunity to realize that the Spirit makes it possible for me to understand the language of someone else's despair, allowing me to offer care and comfort rather than just passing by.

My personal identification with Peter as being a model soul mate is restored to positive status with the account of this event. Once again, I feel the promise of something wonderful ahead of me. God's Spirit will similarly equip me as I need with the strength of faith not only to challenge but also conquer the anxiety and doubt encountered as I follow this new path. It is a new language of the heart, if not the tongue.

Gracias. Danke schön. Merci beaucoup. Thank you.

146

How Do We Get There?
looking at the destination

JOHN 14:1–15

continue to learn and grow as I discover who the troublemaker tenants are and give them their eviction notice. As I do that, I feel calmer and more confident. While there is still the odd "thump in the night", the old house ruckus is gone.

Today's reading from John's record allows me to eavesdrop on a conversation between Jesus and the disciples. Two of the disciples, Thomas and Philip, ask questions that I find surprising—not because the questions are odd, but because the disciples were the ones asking them. There have been a number of times where I think those first followers exhibited the same lack of comprehension I do.

Because of their immediate physical presence with Jesus, I expect them to have had a better understanding and belief in him than my own, yet conversations like this one prove they did not. Actually, their uncertainty serves to validate my non-physical contact with Jesus as being every bit as real and effective as theirs, and they were living and traveling with him. Their doubt strengthens my faith. It shows that my historical displacement from the years when Jesus was here in the flesh is not a disadvantage. In the Bible, Jesus claimed he would always be alive and accessible through the Holy Spirit. I have found that to be the case for me, but I have also found myself susceptible to doubt on a number of occasions, wondering if my experiences with him are products of my imagination. Readings like this one erase such doubts.

The call to believe in Jesus is the same for us all. The men and women who responded before me probably didn't find it any easier to understand the mystery than I do now. The disciple Thomas, for example, echoes a question many people voice today: "Where is this place we are supposed to be going?" He is, of course, asking about Heaven. Like me, Thomas still isn't sure how to get there, since it is not marked on any map or loaded into GPS software. Nor is our logic capable of computing the coordinates Jesus gives.

I don't know what Heaven is exactly, and I have found few words in the Bible describing it in the geographic terms my logic would prefer. Yet I know from my contact with the Holy Spirit that it is a place to which I want to go. I have developed a yearning for it similar to the one I feel for Yorkshire, England, where my father was born and my ancestors lived. It is an intuitive and spiritual connectedness to a place where I do not actually live, though I am directly and intricately a part of the life there. It is a part of me and I am a part of it in a way that is not tangible.

I have felt this bond with Yorkshire ever since I was old enough to understand the stories my father told about his family and childhood. Much later, as an adult, I sought more information about the specific geographic details and his family members. As this information accumulated, so did the intensity of my connection. Eventually, I found myself making a journey to those places where my ancestral roots were anchored.

In talking with friends about this experience, I discovered a few who were adopted as young children and for various reasons were unable to find their family roots. Every one of them told of a gnawing sense of being lost, in varying degrees of intensity, resulting from their sense of belonging to some historical line but not knowing where or what it was.

Thomas and I both want to know where this Heaven is to which we belong. We both want to know how to get there. Jesus gives us one of those upside-down answers by saying that he is the map, and if we believe in him, we know how to get there. I sit and think about that for a while, as I expect Thomas did.

It's not my idea of a road map, but I actually think I'm starting to know what he means.

This sense of connectedness is another positive addition to the Boarding House, now that clearing a lot of the useless junk out has opened some space.

Trust Me
building trust, achievement

he memory of a night of extreme anxiety and exhilarating victory comes back to me after reading these verses. Though the verses are introduced as a message to the church people at Laodicea, I am skewered by the personal relevance for me.

Quite a number of years ago, I enrolled in adult swimming lessons at the YMCA. It was an attempt to challenge my lifelong fear of water any deeper than waist height. I longed to be able to jump into a swimming pool and enjoy the water like most people around me. Many, many times, I sat on a deck while everyone else participated in the fun and refreshment. I often experienced the embarrassment of being the only one who had to confess an aquatic disability. In spite of my regret about this gap in my skill set, I remained poolside, the obstacle of fear still too large to get past.

One winter, however, in a moment of bravado, I enrolled in the swimming class for beginners and challenged the enemy. Most nights, as I approached the water, I searched for that same muster that had persuaded me to sign up, but it rarely revisited me.

I endured the required number of classes, resulting in a marginal easing of fear, and the final night eventually arrived. Graduation involved the students lining up and one by one jumping from the diving board into the deep end of the pool. Though I had manoeuvred myself to the end of the line, my turn to enter the chlorinated depths came well before I was sufficiently steeled for the experience.

Standing on the end of the board, I initiated a comic routine of jokes and one-liners with the instructor and classmates in a desperate attempt to delay confrontation with my fear of the water. Though I had survived until this night, I was sure the water would claim me now. Drowning seemed inevitable.

Attempting to pop the bubble of my fears, the instructor offered words of encouragement. She reminded me of the instructions I'd been given. Then she called out assurances of her assistance if it was required, and pointed to the survival of all the previous jumpers. Could I trust her? I wanted so badly to be able to jump. I didn't want to yield to the call for retreat that was pounding in my chest.

Finally, in exasperation, she gave me permission to return to the side of the pool.

Though only seconds passed, it felt like an interminable passage of time before my toes moved the two inches necessary to leave the diving board. History paused, waiting for me to drop the couple of feet from the board to the water. It seemed like an eternity before my body ascended, the surface of the water breaking to release me. My first gulp of air triggered a race of jubilation into every pore of my body, and I realized that the stranglehold of fear could never again be what it had been.

These words spoken by Christ and recorded in the third chapter of Revelation are calling to me just as that swimming instructor had done. I'd been given instruction; I'd been shown how to do it; I'd been given the examples of others who were successful; I'd been given assurances of help if needed; I'd been given the freedom to make my own decision. The instructor knew what I was facing from the first night's lesson and had calmly given me everything I needed to succeed. She knew the great victory possible to me if I followed through. She was also aware of the fact that it had to be my choice.

Sitting on the board for the night was not an option. Either I could jump into the freedom of conquered fear or I could remain in its grip and walk back to the side of the pool. For weeks, I had been telling people about my class at the YMCA. It impressed everyone who knew of my fear of water and they heaped praise on me for doing this. I enjoyed this new image of myself as a swimmer right up until the moment I took my perch on the end of the diving board. That's when I had to admit that my perception of being a swimmer had not yet been forged into reality. Until I resurfaced from the jump into the deep end, my status was only halfway changed.

Now, in this last book of the Bible, Christ reminds me that halfway is not enough with God. I must not be satisfied with having gotten this far, knowing that a lot people already think I am a changed person. Within me, I know that I keep holding back, hesitating to move forward. Much more is promised to those who listen for his voice and then follow through with what they see and hear. Christ's words push me now much like that swimming instructor did, yet I can also see the sparkle of confident expectation in his eyes, just as the look of anticipation on the swimming coach's face betrayed the sternness of her words ricocheting off those tiled walls.

It's time to jump again.

Project Manager
building community

1 Corinthians 14:6–12

The routine circumstances of my daily life have not changed, yet they no longer have the same abusive effect on me. I must be the one changing. I eagerly look forward to this quiet time each day reading the Bible with my boarder/teacher/friend.

This is the first time, however, that I have come with particular questions already on my mind. Recent readings instructed me to join with others who are similarly calling on God. A light sense of agreement nudged me while reading it. Having now had some time to digest the thought, my mood is a little more cautious. Does this mean I am supposed to go to a church?

My previous ventures to such places have left me more confused and anxious than I was prior to entering. The many books and inserts needed to participate in the worship service have left me bewildered in some churches. Notices and announcements of meetings talk of busyness but don't tell me much about God or Jesus. In others, while there was no such printed regimen, it was obvious that everyone else knew what was expected of them while I sat quite unprepared for each new item on the agenda.

The congregations that included arm-waving routines with singing left me baffled and self-conscious, regardless of whether I was joining in or remaining the single motionless person in the building. The words in the books and sermons often made little or no sense to me—sometimes because those difficult words or unfamiliar concepts were incomprehensible to me, and other times the words were so simple that they lacked enough depth or relevance to help me. In all of these churches, my resulting level of discomfort has kept me from noticing if God was there or not.

The people I have seen in these various churches do not appear to have anything in common with me. The derisive statements I've heard or made about Christians are often confirmed by the way I am made to feel as though I am trespassing. Sitting in a pew or standing in a crowded room for after-service coffee actually accentuates my feelings of aloneness.

My conclusion was that churches did not have what I'm looking for. Therefore I determined that God was not what I wanted, and decided not to return. Is the Bible pointing me back to these churches?

The boarder, whose perspective is always better than mine, helps me find the answer in today's lesson.

These verses illustrate the necessity of using language and words that can be clearly understood. Though every language is meaningful, you will be a stranger to another person without some language in common.

I recall my attempts to learn about God in those churches. Though everyone certainly spoke the same language I did, there was no gain in understanding for me. Somehow, through the choice of vocabulary, the concepts spoken of, and the practices exercised, a language was being used which left me in the dark. These verses point out that a message that's not understood is of no help to anyone, and may even become a barrier.

Today's reading ends with an encouragement to seek and use the gifts of the Spirit to build the church.

Build the church? Those earlier words about building me into a temple return.

Gifts of the Spirit? I'm not sure what gifts are being referred to, or where they are, but a warm glow embraces me as I think of the house-warming gift the Spirit brought to me—opening the meaning and love contained in the words in the Bible. A quick swipe of clarity removes the film of condensation that's keeping me from clearly seeing the connections here.

The Holy Spirit of God sees each of us as being worthy to be a temple. We also have the potential to come together forming a larger, single body, living life abundantly and purposefully in relationship with our Creator. The purpose of the Holy Spirit's gifts is to help and guide us as we become this temple.

Rebuilding me into a temple for the Spirit also gives me the internal characteristics I need to be a vital and integral part of a larger church. I am beginning to see how the various gifts of the Holy Spirit, listed in different ways and times in these Bible readings, are the same ones being used to repair and reequip me. Learning the truth about God is having many wonderful effects on me. It is also clear that this work will involve my own labour, as well as the Spirit's, if I want the changes to continue and be complete.

I do, so it looks as if part of my participation will include joining with others.

This brings some discomfort for me, though, because of my perception of Christians in their churches. I have not been able to speak their "church language," so I have not understood them. But if they are God's people, why hasn't that happened? Aren't these verses saying that it is up to them to find a language I can comprehend?

My unseen teacher lets me dangle in the silence for a while as I contemplate that one.

Soon, my thoughts turn towards seeing those people as temples under construction, the same as I am. Though perhaps further developed, they are not complete, either. Maybe together, like a Habitat for Humanity project, we will build ourselves as we help build each other. God's Spirit will be our project manager. I am beginning to realize that there is some responsibility on me as well as on them in order for us to understand each other.

While I have some apprehension about involvement with a church again, I also, because of what I have experienced so far, feel a tingle of anticipation about what lies ahead. It looks like the project manager will be identifying some more of these gifts and showing me where to find them. I might even be in for a crash course in the language of church building.

"…they shall speak in new tongues…"

Safety Boots
reluctance addressed

1 Corinthians 12:12–31

Some days I feel like a boot that doesn't fit. This is one of them.
A lot of good things have occurred in my life since welcoming the new boarder. These have brought about a number of decisions, resolutions, and effort on my part to live each day differently than how I'd lived before.

The first and most dramatic evidence of my new thinking is the time I've learned to set aside from the busyness of my life to talk with the Spirit and read a few verses of the Bible. This simple change has given me peaceful moments of rest, companionship when I'm feeling alone, new approaches for resolving my fears, and profound discoveries about myself, God, and the world around me. These periods of time have become a vital part of my life because of their regenerative effect on me.

The next most noticeable difference is my involvement in a church. I would never have dreamed such a liaison possible, nor would most people who have known me for any length of time. Contact with this community of God's people has brought to me a more formal understanding of this private experience I've had with the Holy Spirit and the Bible. Church has introduced me to the concept of worship and prayer with other people who, each in their own way, are also acquainted with God.

Through the lyrics of the songs, hymns, and prayer books used in Sunday services, I continue to expand my image of God from my small, personal knowledge of him. I have learned about giving thanks and praise back to God. I feel great after having spent so much time focused only on receiving solutions to my many needs.

All the changes to my thinking have resulted in new actions, both internal and external. My priorities are not the same anymore. Even my patterns of speech are new. I am filled with a sense of wonder and expectation that I've not enjoyed since childhood. Every day feels fresh and promising.

So what do these happy changes have to do with a shoe that doesn't fit? It all starts with a disconcerting question about where I now belong.

I no longer seem to fit within my family in the familiar way I once did, disruptive though it was. Parents, in-laws, siblings, my wife and children are unanimously baffled by the changes in my behaviour patterns. Though delighted by the absence of my customary hardness and surprised by my newfound openness, their reactions to my explanation for the transformation are often expressed in words of suspicion or avoidance. This is no doubt justified by sporadic displays of my old ways that are not yet totally eradicated, but the notion of my turning into a believer and churchgoer seems too much for them to accept. There's no intention on their part to be unkind or unsupportive, but it leaves me feeling separated from them in a way I cannot really articulate. I had always created my own brand of separation through my troubled attitude and behaviour, but now I am actively seeking and following something that is changing all that. I want their approval—instead, I can see that they do not understand.

Certainly I no longer fit with many of my old friends, acquaintances, and coworkers. Their suspicion and derision is much less subtle than it is amongst my family. They seem disappointed as my sharp, sarcastic, and coarse language is gradually washed out of my daily habits. I no longer lead the way with outrageous behaviour at weekend parties or on-the-road tavern visits with coworkers. Their disappointment has turned to suspicion and an awkward form of separation. Ever since the time they learned I was attending church, I've sensed a growing distance between us. Again, it's not intended to hurt me. It's simply a reflection of how different I am becoming to the person these people once knew. The change is not easy for them, or me, to understand.

Though naturally hesitant about what lies ahead, I'm pleased with my newness and convinced that it is what I want. It would be much easier to hold back, but glimpses of the life available to me strengthen my resolve to continue. I am surprised, though, after all the turmoil they have caused me, how reluctant I am to give up the familiar attitudes and behaviour patterns of my past.

The shift in my own priorities adds to my sense of no longer fitting in at otherwise familiar places. My standards for success used to be based on the people I surrounded myself with, but now I'm looking for success within myself. I'm taking the time to absorb the thoughts written in books by popular Christian authors and seeking weekend conferences or workshops where I can learn about the church, spirituality, leadership, and anything else related to God. My appointment calendar now contains weekly meetings of committees involved with the church I now attend. I am starting to see myself as having some worth.

Surprisingly, though, I don't really feel like I fit into the church group, either. There, where everyone is happy and welcoming, my thoughts remind me of past words and actions. I am ashamed of them yet continue to drag them around with me like heavy baggage. I'm not sure how to get rid of them, but I know I want to be a part of the church. I doubt the people I've met in the church would want me if they knew what I once was like. Hopefully these positive people will not find out about my past rejection of them and God. I want to hide this part of my story, and yet this lack of honesty makes me feel uncomfortable.

Thinking of all these places where I don't seem to fit smears me with a sense of loneliness and puzzlement. Where do I fit? Why has Jesus bothered knocking on my door and calling me out if there is no place for me?

As I ask these questions, I feel tempted to give up. The voices of my doubting thoughts are right. I don't belong amongst God's people and I am not like them. There is no place for me.

"But what about me?"

The words abruptly pop my expanding bubble of self-pity. I am aware again of the immediate and loving presence of God's Spirit. I return to the paperback Bible and together we read from the first letter to the Corinthians where Paul talks about the different parts of the body of Christ. The verses embrace me and hold the promise that, in fact, there is a place for me.

I think again of those men and women I've met in church. Maybe their happiness came from an experience like mine. I haven't given much thought to that possibility. Maybe God has helped them in the same way that he's renewing me. This thought reassures me and says that I do belong. Maybe I've just been trying to put the boot on the wrong foot.

Yard Work
corrections and adjustments

MATTHEW 21:18–21, JOHN 15:1–13

Sitting here in the old armchair again, these verses contain the first instance where I'm left wondering if Jesus goofed. This thought actually gives me some comfort.

I've noticed most of Jesus' teaching was done in an agricultural area where everyone was familiar with gardening and crop production, so he often used examples like the one in this story. In this incident, a hungry Jesus comes to a fig tree and, when he sees there is no fruit on it, he causes it to wither away. Did he intend to use his power this way, or did he do it without thinking? This incident seems a bit like the time I kicked the car door after I catching my finger in it. My impatience finds a little company here from someone who has a flawless reputation for patience.

When I read these few verses, I want to see this as a snap response of impatience from him, verging on anger. The tree wasn't ready to provide wholesome nourishment as it was supposed to and his quick retort actually caused it to die instantly. Jesus obviously wasn't going to tolerate such an unproductive existence when it had been set there for a purpose.

Discomfort suddenly seizes me as I think of whether I might be like that tree. What if he judges me the same way? Opportunities come along for me to do or say something that will utilize the new life the Spirit is bringing to me, but then I chicken out, feeling unsure of myself and reluctant to risk a response that may embarrass me. Like that tree, I am not doing what I should. In moments like this, I'm thankful that Jesus has proven he is not about to make such a harsh judgment of me. But why did he of that tree? This does not seem to be a likely action from a man of peace and restoration. Couldn't he fix the tree and save it? Was his harshness an accidental slip, or was it intentional?

For a moment, I wish it was as easy to get rid of some of those remaining volatile aspects of my pride as it was for Jesus to rid that orchard of a non-productive tree.

Yesterday, my impatience surfaced again over what I deemed to be a ridiculous attitude from a business acquaintance. My words were sharp and strong, releasing my own tension but creating it, I think, in the other person. I cannot really claim any productive results from my approach. My point was made, but both of us paid a price. Today, I wish I had found a more positive method of giving feedback to this person. Instead of being embarrassed by acknowledging my belief in the words of Jesus, I am now embarrassed by myself. Did Jesus feel this way after his atypical treatment of the useless tree?

My interest is piqued, thinking perhaps that Jesus and I may share this commonality for emotional outbursts. He has my attention as he proceeds to answer the astonished disciples' question. Their question is not mine, though. They are more interested in how the fig tree died than they are in the reason Jesus did this. He answers their question by telling them about the incredible feats it is possible to perform through prayer if the person praying has enough faith. His words imply that anything can be done if he or she believes in God and holds no doubt about God's will for us. Time has shown me that such a capacity for faith is easier written than accomplished, and I have some distance to go before attaining it.

Even so, his reply side-tracks me. I am also interested in the "how."

I think about my personality traits that continue to embarrass and trouble me. I want to change whatever it is that causes me to treat people abruptly. That's the first demonstration of an undoubting faith I would like to exercise, but it wouldn't take long to write a list of the other things I would like to try next. For instance, I would like to be able to see the folly of some of my actions *before* committing them, instead of after. Jesus' statement also allows my mind to slip into foolishness; would it be possible to use this power to win the lottery, for example? Is that the message Jesus is giving here? He provides a couple of odd examples for the use of this power, I think. Who needs to kill a fig tree or move a hill into the ocean?

Maybe the lesson is not about the availability of authority and power, but the need for responsibility in using them. I'm sure Jesus wants the disciples to understand what they would be capable of doing because of their faith in him. He was showing them how easy it would be to achieve the things they would be tempted to want, sometimes in the spur of the moment. To keep their intentions protected from accomplishing selfish or foolish acts, he told them that their request had to be placed in the envelope of prayer. This would require some earnestness and thought, which also tends to edit out impulsive or misdirected requests.

I have discovered that by the time I formulate my desired objective into the words of a prayer requisition I have been through a process that substantially refines my original intention. Sometimes my request is amplified and expanded, while at other times it is trimmed or eliminated. Putting it in prayer always results in a better request than the one I started with. I lose the temptation to serve only my own needs, and the resulting prayers produce better results than I had hoped for or imagined.

This seems to be an appropriate time to look back on my outburst yesterday and determine whether Jesus goofed in this instance or provided a helpful lesson to me.

So with this in mind I decide to pray. Focusing for a few moments to choose my words results in the decision to ignore my first inclination to ask that I don't have to deal with such people anymore and instead ask for insight into my own behaviour. Next I ask for the capacity to be more patient, to create a positive change in my behaviour.

As I express my thoughts I find myself asking about the condition of this other person—the person I was impatient with. It occurs to me that this person could be troubled in some way and that his aberrant behaviour and language was an unconscious outlet for tension or hurt.

Viewed in this light, my frustration and judgmental retaliation can be seen for what it is—uncaring and selfish. If I had extended the understanding and patience Jesus has shown me, this person and I would have had a very different result from our encounter at the meeting.

My critical judgment of the way Jesus used his power to waste the fig tree rather than renew its vigour and productivity is now reflected in my actions against that person. I wasted an opportunity to pass along what had been given and taught to me. Not only had I wasted the opportunity, but I failed to even see it. My evenings now often include exercising the duties of membership on church committees and groups whose declared mandate is to demonstrate and extend God's love and presence, yet here I missed an easy opportunity to do so.

In fact, to the people who witnessed my impatient behaviour, I set a provocative example to the contrary. No special capacity is required to be impatient. The world is already full of people willing to cut down an unproductive tree. By that standard, Jesus should have made firewood out of me, too.

This session has brought me around to seeing that some aspects of my attitude and behaviour can indeed be likened to a tree that is not fulfilling its purpose. These attitudes need to wither and die, just as that fig tree did.

Needless to say, I no longer think that Jesus goofed. Instead I think I'll go see if there's enough faith in me to wither some of those useless trees in the orchard of my attitude.

A horticultural theme appears in the second reading as John records another of Jesus' training sessions with the disciples. In this one, Jesus is explaining to them how vital their relationship is to him.

Here he uses grapes, another familiar crop, in his analogy. The disciples would have understood the necessity and nature of constant care required by grape vines for them to be productive. They would have known that one of the most vital management practices in a vineyard was skilful pruning of the branches on each individual vine. Any branches that were poorly located, damaged, or without flower had to be cut off so that they wouldn't drain nutrient energy from the vine. Vineyard owners learned to distinguish and remove these branches so that the rest of the vine would flourish. The pruned branches were only useful as firewood.

Using this well-understood practice of crop management, Jesus likened the disciples and all other people to branches on a grape vine. He described himself as the vine rooted in the soil. He reminded them like the vine is the essential life support of the branches, he is our essential connection to God. Without the vine, the branches cannot live. He continued to unfold the image by saying that by believing in him, God acts like a vine keeper, providing constant care and pruning for us to be healthy and productive.

Once again a small chord of fear vibrates inside me. If I too, am like a branch, is there a chance I will be pruned off because of poor productivity? This is a chilling thought, but my friend the boarder encourages me to move on in my thoughts to see how these stories fit into the analogy of the Boarding House and help explain how harmful traits are being removed from me.

I picture a typical grapevine branch and notice that it has many even smaller branches and shoots forking off from it. By visualizing myself as a branch, each of those smaller shoots could represent the different aspects of my personality and resulting attitudes and behaviours. The good and the bad are all included. It makes for a full and cluttered image but I can now see how the vine keeper would work.

The branches labelled jealousy, doubt, and anger will be targets of the pruning shears. The ones labelled love, sharing, and empathy will remain, allowed to grow unhindered. The first three affect me much the same way that leaf blight or fungi would affect the health of the whole branch on an actual grapevine. If the vine is to reach its full potential, these unhealthy branches must be pruned. If certain attitudes and habits of mine are going to cause me trouble and pain, they must be given up so that I can be renewed.

Before my introduction to Jesus, I was a very full branch, full to the point of choking. Some of these branches represented extra stuff with no inherent goodness or badness, but they were an unnecessary drain on my time and energy, and therefore were unproductive and restraining. The rest of the fullness contained harmful and destructive shoots, as well as potentially productive ones. I had an attitude of arrogance, thinking that my opinion was the only correct one, which was an excellent example of a single facet of my personality that affected the rest of me very negatively. Thought of as a branch, it needed to be pruned so that I could grow and produce a healthy crop of activity with my life.

The disciples were told that the teaching and corrections Jesus gave them is the pruning action of God. This makes for an odd mental image, until I think of how many changes have resulted in my life because of what I've read in the Bible or experienced from praying. Those verses and words don't resemble any pruning shears I have seen, but they certainly trimmed off a lot of bad stuff and made a difference in how I feel and act. Without that care the tangle would have continued to grow, choking off any potential for a healthy life.

If I am like a branch on a grapevine, I want the vine keeper that Jesus talks about to care for me.

Remembering the obvious state of neglect in the yard and garden around the image of the house on that first visit makes me thankful the boarder arrived with pruning shears and a green thumb.

Construction Company
working with others

I said I wanted a new life and my life sure is changing, day by day. Awareness of the renovation that is underway on my thoughts and feelings is at the top of my mind everyday.

Paul, like Jesus' disciples, teaches in this chapter of Romans that there are specific things God hopes we will achieve. In order for them to occur, we must develop ourselves in particular ways. This implies change. I am a typical human and easily fall into familiar patterns of living. I will even rally to a defensive mindset if some of my patterns are threatened. This in itself may not be wrong, but in moments of honest insight I can see that a lot of my adopted ways are not worth defending.

Judging by the first line in today's reading, my boarder is not about to assume I have learned all I need to know about building temples yet. When I first encountered Jesus, I was desperate. I wanted changes to occur in the circumstances and people around me, assuming I would feel better when everything met my expectations. I wanted someone to just wave a magic wand and make it all better.

Since then, I have been shown that many of the changes I deemed necessary could have their start from within me. That surprised me but as I stopped long enough to listen to the Spirit, albeit reluctantly initially, the truth of that finally became apparent to me as well.

I was introduced to the concept of "temple building" and the renovation got underway. I liked what that started to do for me.

Paul's writing here in Romans further encourages me to truly understand the source and purpose of these changes. He uses the example of a human body to explain how all believers in God are united and related to Jesus and each other as individual parts of the same body.

Though all are human beings living on the same blue planet, each person remains unique from all the others. The Holy Spirit is not a cookie cutter. Educational backgrounds are different, as are social and financial circumstances. Good health and physical fitness are some people's characteristics, while others face difficult challenges or deficits. Warm, loving families and friends have nourished some, while many others have suffered neglect, betrayal, or abuse. Happy, carefree lives contrast to heavily burdened ones. Steady, uneventful life experiences are as common as those interrupted by crisis and disappointment, shattered by a problem relationship or elevated by great achievement. Thousands of languages are spoken. Some see God as male, some as female, others knowing God as existing beyond gender.

The only thing they have in common is every man, woman, youth, and child in this group has met and experienced God's love. That extraordinary experience binds them together in a way that no creed, mission statement, or nationality could. Each person has been rescued or transformed by God through Jesus and the Holy Spirit. It is a love that transcends human definition and experience.

Functioning like a complex network of arteries and veins, God's Holy Spirit delivers sustaining love to each and every person who asks for it. This single source of love connects the many people together and holds them as distinct parts of a single body. Each of these parts completes the whole, and the whole completes each part. Together they are building God's temple.

The Holy Spirit is showing me that I can be one of those parts. Paul states that God is able to transform us on the inside through a refreshing cleansing and healing of our mind. This will enable us to know what is right and whole in the thoughts, words, and actions of our daily lives. This is what I am experiencing as the result of the renovation.

Some weeks ago this troubled me, sounding like serious meddling with my inner works. I still don't find the scrutiny of my many thoughts, words, and deeds very comfortable, but it is working.

I was making a lot of mistakes in the way I was building my spiritual home. I did it my way, but there were strong indications that the result of the life I was building would probably destroy rather than sustain me. There was a hollow space deep inside me where I cried, "There must be another way." The Holy Spirit accessed this place, though it cannot be found on any chart of the human anatomy. I think this will be the room where the Spirit will settle once the Boarding House renovation is complete.

When praying and open to the Spirit's presence, I am able to think differently. Thoughts of anger—thoughts that tempt, frighten, and twist—have no power in these times.

The framework of this time is formed from promise, hope, acceptance, and expectation. From here, I am able to see how the loose, chaotic way I was living my life only produced a lot of accumulating clutter. Prior to meeting Jesus, the door was barricaded by my defensive unbelief and my junk. The painful, disruptive relationships that resulted with the events and people around me were the natural consequences.

The boarder, God's Spirit, continues to encourage me through my mood swinging between doubt and hope—convincing me that I am a part of God's people—a temple builder.

Now, I want to be like the people Paul describes in these verses. I want to be like Paul and the other men and women I'm reading about in the Bible. I want that hope and that strength of faith and clarity of purpose they exude. I want to have the cleanliness of heart and mind suitable to be a temple or dwelling place for the Spirit of God. I want the smile on my face also to be in my heart and on Jesus' face when he looks at me. I'm describing a different me than I was when this started and in fact I do already feel lighter and freer than ever before.

My friends' and family's reactions are unexpected though. I am feeling better and changing my attitude positively, yet it seems that I continue to concern them somewhat by making them unsure of who I am now. As I think about this though, maybe their reaction is good news. Something noticeable must actually be taking place. What am I becoming?

Today's lesson provides an answer for me.

Birthday Suit
adjusting to the new image

1 CORINTHIANS 14:20–25, EPHESIANS 4:25–32

He got me again. Sometimes it seems Paul was thinking about me before writing his letters to those first members and builders of the church. I read these two brief excerpts today with my favourite boarder. In them, Paul again parallels the thoughts and events in my life at this very moment. I have been wondering lately about how I appear to other people. Within my own mind, I often feel quite naked. A lot of the time, to compensate for feeling that way, I intentionally put on a camouflage suit. Maybe the time has come to strip it off.

Camouflage suit? The term tries to explain something I've noticed since making an effort to experience life outside the Boarding House. It describes the way I've been presenting myself to other people as I try to put what I'm learning to use. The family and friends around me are noticing the changes in my behaviour and language because of the way I've abandoned, slowly, my characteristic emotional abrasiveness.

I realize that the new people I meet, now that I am trying to attend a church regularly, only see me as I am today—not as the person I was. I am acutely aware of what I was like before the renovation started and to be truthful, embarrassed by it. It is also quite clear to me that I'm not completely changed yet—there are some things that still have to be worked on. What I show you of me today is true and accurate though at the same time I try to keep the junk stuff hidden from view—thus the term camouflage.

The uber, over-the-top, locking system design in the Boarding House resulted from my attitude and preference for wanting to be private and untouchable. I have come to realize though that it was always penetrable by a few individuals who were unfazed by my rebuffs. They wanted to help me in spite of my self-imprisonment, and a few of them—though not all—believed in God and Jesus Christ. Though I was not always appreciative or a gracious host, their presence and example kept me from coming right off the rails and in the case of my co-worker, pointed me to the first step in this life renewing experience.

So-called "grunge" would be the fashion term to appropriately describe my attitude and lack of respect in the past, but as peace and even happiness fills the new space within me I have become more aware of how I appear to people. I want to be more open, inviting other people to know me—the Boarding House. What do I now want them to see of me?

Longer term acquaintances, now see the same basic image. I have somehow "discovered" God and am now involved in church attendance and activities. Some of them find this new image of me laughable, while others think it laudable.

This image is not complete, though, because I share with none of them the incredible activity of my times in prayer with the paperback Bible and the details of what has been going on in my heart. I am afraid they will reject me—though with some of them that might be better for me.

There is no intent to be dishonest or misleading. Discomforting, nagging thoughts—the whining voices of previous tenants protesting their eviction—return now and then. Though the renovation is going well, I realize I am a bit inconsistent in my behaviour. Some days, through uncertainty, combined with embarrassment and awkwardness, I'm not sure who I am myself. The functionality of the living quarters in the Boarding House is dramatically improving but I am keenly aware of the chaos it once contained and so are some of the people around me. I hold some fears about the permanence of these changes and I'm afraid that other people will also question the credibility of the renovation.

When I am with people who have known or worked with me for some time, I try to pretend that I am still the rough and tumble me. When I am with the new church people, I try to pretend there is no rough and tumble me. The camouflage appearance has helped me through this adjustment phase but it is starting to feel uncomfortable and dishonest.

A few days ago, a close friend confided to me the fear threatening him; his wife was about to undergo a hasty surgical procedure to confirm or dispel suspicions of a life-threatening disease. His conversation surprised me because neither he nor I were prone to discussing intimate emotion. Fortified by the Spirit's prodding, I went and sat in a hospital hall with him the next day through the excruciating time before the suspected diagnosis was confirmed. Words and tears poured out of me as I attempted to comfort him and give him some hope. I prayed with and for him. I knew there was no place for a camouflage suit during those moments.

If clothes really do make the person, then perhaps Paul's letters are telling me it is time to change the wardrobe and display the birth of new life in the Boarding House.

Material List
the need for valuable differences

Romans 14:17–19

In today's letter, Paul admonishes the congregation of Christians in Rome. It appears that some disagreement was stirred up there about the appropriateness of eating certain foods. This created troublesome results for people both in the congregation and among those outside it who observed them and their behaviour.

Paul succinctly makes the point that Christ came to teach us about God's Kingdom, not God's kitchen. He is trying to get this group to focus not on their differences but on their common relationship and potential with Jesus. With these few words, he warns us about tripping over issues of belief, often formed with good intention but usually contrary to the intention of God's Word.

My contemplation of these short verses reminds me , for some strange reason, of a particular bowl of Christmas fruit punch. One of the few jobs in the kitchen entrusted to me for festive family meals, beyond mashing the potatoes, is preparing the punch. The first time I was entrusted with creating this culinary delight, I considered the possibility that the list of ingredients provided to me might contain errors.

Apple cider, canned raspberries, tea, orange juice, lemons, limes, and cloves. How on earth could such divergent flavours, textures, and aromas ever come to any common good? I was tempted to leave out a couple of items being aware of their tartness, but in acknowledgement of my culinary deficiencies, decided to trust the wisdom on the recipe card.

Looking at the ingredients in the blender returned me briefly to my original reservations about their compatibility. Almost reluctantly, I flipped the switch. A flurry of motion and colour followed and seconds later the freckled, homogenous-coloured liquid was ready to pour over the ice block in the punch bowl. I had to admit that it looked okay. It even had a tantalizing aroma, distinct from the sharpness of some of the individual ingredients. Before long, to my surprise, the taste-testers of the party were voicing acclaim. Something appetizingly new had been created from the apparently disparate ingredients. If each had been left on its own, it would have remained unchanged and, in some instances, unused because of its questionable appeal.

The boarder is at work again. I now see a distinct similarity between this odd memory and Paul's church building work.

Just as various ingredients, both complimentary and contradictory, were mixed together to create something new—the punch, so does the universal church or "temple" as Paul refers to it.

The building of the church starts with a list of varied materials as well because it is made up of individual people—like me even. Everyone who comes and is built into it has a unique personality and story. Each has his or her own talents and interests to add. Each will also contain unique needs or struggles. Some are confident and happy, others are hurting or lost.

These are the materials that God chooses to build the church.

Through reading the Bible I have come to realize that the process of getting a new life starts with a renovation that makes us first a suitable home for the Spirit (and ourselves), getting rid of what hinders us and enhancing what maximizes our potential. This then progresses to developing each of us to become a part of the bigger "temple"—the body of God's people.

My renovation so far has been very private and graphic but I think that like there are many different people and needs, there are many different experiences possible for an introduction to God.

As we grow individually and together we will take our new found hope wherever we go, letting those who see us see what change is possible for them and those places.

Like the ingredients of the punch, some of us don't look or feel like we are good building material or belong but God knows otherwise. It looks to me like he wants us all in his building project.

Break Time

time to assess and recharge

ACTS 1:12–14, HEBREWS 13:11–13

Strong emotions are stirred up in me by these three simple verses in the first chapter of Acts. The first emotion is empathy for the group of people assembled in this upper room in Jerusalem. The meeting takes place immediately following the moment of ascension I read a while ago, when Jesus gave his last instructions and then physically left the earth.

My expectation is that it would be like a cross between the two most familiar types of family gatherings I have often attended—funerals and weddings. The atmosphere must have been ping-ponging between the opposite moods found at those events.

On one hand, their dear friend, brother, and son had been executed only six weeks earlier, following a series of rather extraordinary, fearful events that saw their own lives turned upside down and changed forever. On the other hand, mind-boggling, joyful encounters had occurred in which this man they knew and loved proved beyond doubt that he had returned to life from death. He had told them he would do so, but understandably they weren't prepared when it actually happened. As if this wasn't enough to grapple with, they are also probably still stunned by the betrayal and suicide of a former member of the inner group— Judas. Can you imagine the buzz of conversations in this room?

The disciples present are all named, some of these names I have never seen mentioned before and until this reading, it never occurred to me to question whether Jesus had siblings. My focus on him has been very narrow, and this revelation about brothers is immensely interesting. I wonder if his brothers and sisters teased him the way mine did. This thought adds to my seeing his humanness.

Given the criticism so often heard about the role of women in the social context of Jesus' lifetime, it is interesting to see here that women were an integral part of the team who worked with him and were present at this time. I also find it gratifying to see that his mother is still present and active in this group. It implies to me that he has had the benefit of a good relationship with his mother and that she has been involved in his work. This is a precious gift not all people are able to enjoy. It makes me think of my own relationship with my mother.

These verses create warm feelings in me. I find this situation very relatable and reassuring in contrast to the loneliness that sometimes haunts me. The apostles in this scene draw me close and I feel included in the group. This reading has somehow reduced the physical and historical distance separating me from them, allowing me to share their experience. This sensation is enhanced even further when Luke talks about how this group frequently gathered to pray. This feels good. I would like to be able to do this with all my family and friends.

During my time as a participant in the Mad Parade, I laughed in scorn at the mere suggestion of prayer and could become downright derisive towards anyone who actually practiced it. My attitude has changed dramatically. No longer do I see prayer as a foolish weakness. Prayer has become the call home I want to make to find out what is going on and be reassured that I am not alone. I want to say thanks for everything sent to me, and I need to acknowledge those times when I goof up. I need this daily connection so that I don't wander off and get lost again by doing everything my own way. It's a direct line where a warm welcome awaits me twenty-four hours a day. Sometimes that welcome adds to my day, and other times it saves it.

The animation of my prayers and Bible readings gives me a sense of belonging to this family of brothers, sisters, parents, and friends in this gathering. Jesus is the reason they form a family.

In Luke's account, this group is doing what I and many others have trivialized and ignored and yet need so badly. They trust what Jesus has told them and are sharing and living that example with each other. It is easy to see the difference it makes in their lives. They are enjoying the embrace of belonging to God's family through each other—just as Jesus showed them.

The invitation to be a part of that family is extended to all of us through the Bible. If we accept, is God ready and willing to enter into the lives of every individual person in need, to remove those prongs that stab at our hearts and minds?

The Bible states that it is not necessary for us to live in the hopeless states of confusion, fear, loneliness, or addiction that dominate and destroy so many of us. The thought crosses my mind that if God dispensed new lives from a booth like the lotteries do with tickets, there would be massive line-ups extending through malls and around the block at every convenience store. People would camp overnight to be first in line. Signs and posters would proclaim his name on public transit vehicles and stations. He would be the talk of the town. But that's not how it works.

I think that as simple as I understand the terms are, God's work is very difficult to receive, not because of a flaw or intention on God's part, but because of our attitude. It is hard to separate ourselves from our own understanding of life long enough to touch God's.

As I look around, I can see most of our society—through its schools, magazines, laws, medical practices, billboard posters, television shows, banks, governments, and business practices—either denies God's existence or ignores it. These are the media from which we learn about ourselves. But look what they show us!

The busyness of our lives, combined with the events and teaching we are exposed to everyday, gives us little evidence or opportunity to know that God exists. It's not an exaggeration to say that most of the images and messages we are exposed to daily deny God's existence.

True, many people admit in embarrassed tones that they believe in a supreme being or power which can manipulate the weather or save them in a moment of crisis. Very few, however, think there is a Creator of life who cares enough to help us sort out the hurts that haunt our minds or assault our bodies.

As a society, it seems like we have lost contact with a belief in a source and reason for being. There is little hope or purpose to be found in the declarations of theorists who claim we are nothing more than the result of an explosion of cosmic dust and gases. There isn't much comfort to be found in the assertions of evolutionists who explain our existence through a complicated process of shape-shifting. First from life forms that plopped out of the oceans and later swung through trees before becoming cave dwellers and finally the refined social specimens we are today. Most of our public institutions don't support the claim that we are intelligently, purposefully created beings, and popular opinion doesn't encourage exploration of that possibility.

If this is so, how can we get to know and stay in touch with God? It looks to me like today's verses, from Paul's letter to the Hebrews, hold an important clue to discovering the answer to that question.

He begins by reminding this group of Christians how the old practice of blood sacrifices, offered to redeem sins, were prepared for the temple outside the city, away from the commerce of daily life. It was an action of belief and needed to be done with an attitude of holiness and worship, free from distractions.

He goes on to say that Jesus gave up his life as a replacement for those sacrifices in a similar manner, away from the influence of unbelief and contrary to the standards of secular logic. We are urged to similarly step away from societal interests and values in order to understand the example Jesus gave.

So if I refuse or fail to regularly step outside of the boundaries defined by undiscerning conformity to the logic expressed all around me everyday, I won't be able to open my mind and heart to recognize and communicate with God.

Sports have regular timeouts so that participants can catch their breath and prepare for the next demand on them. Tournaments, wars, and businesses all have structured breaks to provide their participants time to stand back and rest, reassess, adjust, and reorganize. Conversation with God—prayer—is such a timeout. Faith In God, which makes that possible, is a good tenant that belongs in the Boarding House.

In these readings, Jesus reminds those Hebrews—and me—how to access these timeouts. Jesus knew how important it is for us to know God. He died as a sacrificial offering so that we could. That should be all the prompting needed to make time for regular timeouts to say thanks and see what God has to say.

Blow the whistle.

Man's Best Friend
dependable, enjoyable, valuable

JOHN 14:25–26

These two verses from John 14 quote from one of the many teaching sessions Jesus had with the disciples. The passage quickly brings to mind how my impression of God's Spirit has changed since our first introduction. As my understanding has changed and expanded, so has my perception of the Spirit's role.

Thinking back to the time in the hallway of the house where we first met, I remember seeing a silent figure wrapped in light brown material, like a monk, in the background. There were no distinguishable facial features or movements of any kind. As Jesus departed from the scene, leaving only the two of us, I was somewhat apprehensive and unsure of how I felt about this person. I had just experienced the thrill of discovering the reality of Jesus, and then he was gone, leaving me with this substitute. I felt a bit awkward and disappointed.

My apprehension, as much as the image before me, formed my first expectation of my future boarder. I thought this person would be a religious police officer, sent to bring discipline to one of the "bad boys" and file reports on my behaviour.

This first encounter was the one and only time I ever "saw" the Spirit. After the initial image of an arresting officer, I went through a brief period of picturing the Spirit as one of those live puppeteers who would control my actions and thoughts, but this faded quickly with the realization that I continued to be quite capable of foolish and harmful acts. This image was replaced with that of a leather-aproned construction worker who was cheerfully engaged in the necessary task of restructuring the interior of the Boarding House. This depiction was occasionally supplemented by the comforting image of a loving grandparent, freely pouring out for me the wisdom and understanding gained from a rich lifetime of experience. These personified images reflect my growing confidence and comfort with the presence of God. We moved rapidly from those first awkward moments to the warmth and trust of intimate friendship. This friendship, I am happy to say, saved, reshaped, and continues to build my life.

Today yet another sense of the Spirit's personality comes to me in the form of an image from my favourite childhood story—that of the medieval legend, Robin Hood and the band men and women with him.

The image, based on illustrations and movies I have seen, is of two characters from this story: a large robust man and a capable-looking yet dignified woman. The woman's name is Maude, and she is Lady Marian's friend and lady-in-waiting. In her role, she quietly remains in the background through the story but is always present to serve and protect Marian. Usually she is called upon to take care of Marian's practical needs, but there are several occasions when her duty calls for absolute dedication and commitment as she accompanies her mistress into an assortment of situations. She is an accurate and appropriate representation of the nature of the Spirit's service.

Though there are several more exciting characters in the story of Robin Hood, I have always been impressed with the quiet focus and rock-solid dependability of this young woman. I have felt this same unconditional love and care from the Spirit.

The second character—the man—is known as Little John. He is much more involved in the story, so it's easier to know him better. This hulking giant of a man is fully qualified to be a soldier when the fight against corruption requires physical battle, but the gentle actions of his heart and mind demonstrate that there is more to him than brute strength. He is dedicated to the cause of justice that motivates Robin Hood. Like the other members of the band, he is also protective of Robin and does everything to the best of his abilities to serve Robin and his work.

He directs these talents with the same unselfish compassion to serve all the other members of the band, and anyone else they encounter in their travels. He shares his time, humour, zest for life, and knowledge to build up each member of the group. He is a trustworthy confidant and the first to come to the defense of anyone in danger. Whether he is robustly enjoying the gifts of life, flamboyantly challenging the unjust forces of authority, carefully binding the wounds of an injured comrade, patiently teaching new skills to a young man, or gently cradling a motherless fawn, Little John can be trusted implicitly. In his company, there is safety and a full appreciation of life.

As a boy, I longed to have a friend like Little John. As an adult however, the closest I came was my dog. What a wonderful treat it has been to find that all the idealism portrayed in fiction and dog food commercials has actually come true through God's promise of the Holy Spirit. All and more than I ever hoped for or dreamed of has been experienced in this friendship.

I don't think that the Spirit actually is a silent, hooded monk or a construction worker (or an Irish Setter for that matter). I doubt the Spirit looks like a grandparent or a cop. It is also unlikely that God's Spirit bears much physical resemblance to Maude or Little John. But the Bible readings, combined with my experiences, have given me these personalized representations and through them a tangible understanding of how God is present with me, and the practical loyalty with which he loves me.

Testing
facing temptation

LUKE 22:39–46

Today I am again struck by a sense of belonging to this group, just as I was to the one gathered at the upper room meeting a few days ago. That was very real to me, allowing me to identify with them and share in their emotional circumstances. This time, though, the sense comes to me through a powerful new awareness of Jesus as a man, as opposed to the often held view of him as a divine superman who was not from this planet, and therefore not really affected by life as we are. I suppose this is a baffling threshold for everyone who hears about Jesus. Is he human or isn't he?

In other reading I have discovered that the answer given by theologians is that he is both—fully. I have not yet been able to grasp what that seemingly contradictory answer means. The closest I come is through the shallow comparison of Jesus to the comic book hero Superman.

Like the citizens of Metropolis in that storyline, most of my encounters with Jesus have left me as the benefactor of Supermanesque feats of power and goodwill. Like Lois Lane, who overlooked the value of the mild-mannered Clark Kent (Superman's earthbound persona), I am so enthralled with the out-of-this-world super man that I pay little attention to the flesh and blood Jesus, son of a faithful young mother and tradesman father.

This reading sharply brings my focus to the humanness of Jesus. This is no emotionally detached and invincible superhero standing in the garden a couple of hours before his arrest.

The person I see here is a confident yet nervous man, fully aware of the fact that the departure and betrayal of his friend means that degradation, torture and his physical death are imminent. This would terrify me if I were in his place, draining me of confidence and hope. He was about to die because of the message of love God wanted him to give to us. Luke describes him as being in agony.

That doesn't sound like a guy who is impervious or willing to hide behind the super powers he has displayed when helping other people. He is facing the challenge head on with the same vulnerabilities as me.

So what does he do? He tells the disciples to pray that they will not be overcome by temptation, then goes off amongst the trees to pray by himself.

What will they be tempted to do? Probably the same as me—forget that the strength to face great threats and fears in life will come from having faith in God. Without that faith, despair and anger can take control and bring about defeat. I know that, I was there.

I think Jesus is demonstrating here how to most effectively respond to situations that will test my faith. This whole scene is a reminder that life is not always like a fairy tale with a happy ending and easy decisions. Life situations will test my faith and trust in God. Some decisions will be made in dramatic circumstances as in this reading but there will be many other, more subtle ones on a daily basis that will be equally important, such as how I treat other people; my response when the choice comes in the guise of a harmless fulfillment of a private desire; whether I am honest in my workplace practices; how I extend grace and forgiveness to the people around me.

Facing the test, he removed himself from the logic of the situation and gets into a conversation with God—expecting a response.

In all the accounts I have read about Jesus, it is obvious he understands human vulnerability and limitations and cared about how difficult life could be for us. He faced the same challenges ordinary men and women do to show us that we can challenge and overcome too. He was not exempted from any of the tests I face. His super powers did not get him through them. His only advantage was the faith he says we are all capable of having.

Like Jesus, my life has value and a purpose, whether I see it clearly or not. Reading the Bible has given me a new one and shown me that it is true for everyone else as well. My faith in God will actualize that purpose.

Full Tank
how to keep growing

Acts 1:1–15

Today is the third time I've come to verses written about this particular timeframe of Jesus' life. I am a bit excited because I've learned that rereading a particular section usually produces yet another treasure of information. It is fascinating how these verses can have multiple layers of meaning and relevance—revealed one at a time each time I read them.

Today's verses, from the record titled Acts, expand the time envelope on both sides of Jesus' physical departure from the world.

Jesus' directive for the disciples to wait catches my attention. After all the time they've spent with Jesus—learning from him; suffering through the anxiety, fear, and reality of his death; and then experiencing the shock of seeing him again after his resurrection—these people are now told they still have to wait for the baptism of the Holy Spirit before they are to carry on with the job Jesus trained them to do.

I wonder why, after all they've done, the disciples are not immediately given the company of God's Spirit. The Bible makes it clear that the Holy Spirit comes to dwell in each person who responds with a welcome reception to God's tap on the shoulder. Surely these men had done that. Like me though I suppose, they didn't know anything about the Holy Spirit.

Those men, and the women who worked with them, endured tremendous challenges and opposition to get the message out to other people, ultimately including me, though I doubt any of them thought their work would reach this far into the future. History describes the cost of social and physical abuse the early followers of Jesus paid to deliver the message they were commissioned to take to the world. But they did their job and made it possible for people through the ages since to know about Jesus and what he came to do for us.

Credited by modern scholars as being the founder of Christianity as we know it today, Paul met Jesus in a dramatic introduction some five years *after* Jesus was crucified. About thirty years old at the time, Paul was actively persecuting people who believed in Jesus. This encounter triggered a life change and Paul spent the next thirty years living and teaching about his reflections and insights resulting from that meeting. His letters, written not to make a Bible but to help the churches he established deal with the problems they encountered, were gathered and assembled in the years following his death. He was the first person to demonstrate the practical application of belief and faith in Jesus to the masses. This was the beginning of what we know as the Christian church.

Luke, another writer whose work is significant in the New Testament, also probably did not meet Jesus during his thirty years on earth. Luke was highly educated and trained as a physician. At some point he met Paul and subsequently traveled around the Roman Empire on missionary activities with him.

After Paul's death, Luke became a church leader in the region where he lived. Approximately fifty years after Jesus died, Luke decided to put his academic and evangelistic skills to the task of writing an accurate record of Jesus' work and the birth of the early church. In the introduction to his work, he states that his intention was to combine the best of the narratives already written at the time with the existing oral tradition about Jesus. Luke's understanding and personal experience provided the binding agent of validity for such a project.

His work reaffirmed the inclusiveness of the Christian message for all people regardless of social, political, cultural, or ethnic differences. He placed an emphasis on the active, guiding role of the Holy Spirit wherever faith in Jesus existed.

The uniqueness of Paul and Luke also applies to all other biblical writers. Each of them based their accounts on personal experiences, knowledge, and their relationship with God directly or indirectly.

Many different personalities and educational backgrounds were involved. Does that mean each one turned the story with his or her own emphasis to satisfy personal interest, putting accuracy and credibility at risk? Or was each one's particular understanding the very reason God worked through those individuals?

We all have different preferences and needs that must be met before we become receptive to communication. It is safe to assume God knows of our assorted social and intellectual needs and preferences and therefore sent the same message through different personalities, vocabularies and languages. That way, no one had to be left out through misunderstanding. The integrity of each writer's work is assured through the guidance of the Holy Spirit, who also guides the readers of their writings.

The Bible's message is vital if we are to understand who we are and why we are here. As I am discovering, each of my reading passes uncovers a different function and result. The first for me was to put into motion the changes necessary to provide a suitable residence for the Spirit. Like Paul prior to his meeting with Jesus, most of my values and actions before entering this experience were not complementary to the example Jesus presented for us.

The act of changing, contrary to our commonly held negative or resistive attitude towards change, is an utterly wonderful experience, brimming with rewards for those who choose to engage in its renewal. Each of those who accept the opportunity will describe a unique experience, and yet I expect we will recognize the activity of transformation in one another's stories as having come from the same source.

I know that God's Spirit moved in to start the renovation, though I am fully aware there is more yet to come. I find it impossible to define this awareness in more specific terms. I can see and hold this feeling in my heart more easily than in the logic of my intellect.

How does my experience compare to that of the disciples? Nothing I've read indicates they were confronted by a personal crisis in the way I was, but the few details provided are enough to leave me with the impression that they were ordinary people, carrying concerns, frustration, or embarrassment about their shortcomings and problems the same as anyone today. Jesus called them anyway, maybe even because of their vulnerabilities, and worked in them through the uniqueness of their lives. I know this to be true because of what he is doing in me.

But they were chosen to be *the* disciples. Surely their intense training developed their knowledge and experience far more than I could expect for myself, and therefore they should be ready for the Spirit to take up immediate residence. However, the record shows that this was not the case. In this they seem to be no different to me.

Nothing I have read explains the need for them to wait. Perhaps they needed a pause to do some additional thinking about what was yet to come. Maybe they needed a little more time to absorb the significance of the events of the preceding weeks.

The disciples' fear and timidity immediately following Jesus' death contrasts sharply with recordings of their later actions. The Bible tells us that the difference is due to Pentecost, the day the Holy Spirit moved into each of them.

In his talks and stories, Jesus taught about the effects that faith in God would have on our lives. In one particular story, he likens us to earthenware jugs. Jesus identifies the intention of God, as the potter, to fill the jugs—us—with the Spirit.

My understanding of this teaching is based in my own experience. I have the capacity to gather and contain knowledge. If I am not filled in a discriminate manner with valuable and useful guidance and discernment, I am open to whatever we are exposed to from this world, which at best is incomplete knowledge, and at worst, harmful or worthless refuse.

In our contemporary culture, rather than using jugs as the analogy, two syringes were used. One is filled with a vaccine to prevent polio and the other contains heroin—one is capable of dispensing protection, the other the horrors of addiction. Imagine the difference each of these syringes could make in your life, depending on which one is injected into you. God knows that left to our own choices, we are apt to fill up with the wrong choice, unaware of the danger and damage which invades the life of a person who gradually fills up with garbage rather than the clean fullness of God.

Before leaving them, Jesus told the disciples that they were not yet completely filled with what would protect them and be served through them. Today's passage delivers the same message to me that those disciples received. It also reminds me of what I was filling my spiritual home with and the looming disaster that was leading to. The pause called for in Scripture reminds me that my way is probably not God's way.

Those disciples stayed together as a group, comforting each other, praying and waiting, proceeding when and where God's Spirit led them. I think I am well advised to do the same.

I reread the verses before resuming my schedule for the day and find a comforting yet humorous detail I missed on first reading. Those two men in white materialized from nowhere and spoke to the disciples, leaving them with valuable information, direction, and a question or two about exactly what had happened to them. I am not the only one who receives very real, helpful, and unexplainable appearances of things and people, but it looks as though I'm in good company.

Two Shall Be One
the presence of spouses, partners, best friends

1 Corinthians 12:1–6

In this age of discounts, coupons, and sales, this title—Two Shall Be One—heralds a special bargain.

After previous reflections about faithful friends and companions, this reading is another of those perfect coincidences. My wife is celebrating her birthday today. The reading mentions the gifts of the Holy Spirit. My assumption is that I will learn more about what the Holy Spirit does to help me, but instead my thoughts wander and become focused on my own "two-shall-be-one."

This phrase is found in the Scriptures and used in most marriage ceremonies. At my wedding, it was only a phrase to me. I had little more than disdain for the church and anything it represented. I was only there because my young bride-to-be wanted to be married in the church she had attended as a child with her family. We stood that night before a church minister who had put up a great deal of resistance before consenting to perform the ceremony.

His challenge to us had become a joke amongst my friends and an embarrassment to our families. Though I didn't realize it at the time, it was also the first time God prodded me into serious thought about what I believed.

During an appointment with him, the minister had quickly expressed his disapproval of our marriage because of our premarital pregnancy and his opinion that we were still little more than children ourselves. After a drawn out and awkward conversation, he finally offered us a deal. If we promised to attend church regularly from that point onward and participate in its functions, he would perform the service for us. We were to consider this overnight and call him back the following day with our answer.

The easy route around this obstacle was to agree to his terms but then carry on with our lives just as we had been doing. That was the unanimous intention of all concerned as we discussed the matter around the kitchen table later that night. I would be the one to call the minister and confirm our "commitment to the church."

The next morning, however, found me wrestling with a whole gamut of issues and emotions. I didn't feel right about lying to this man, in spite of my less than charitable evaluation of him for his conditional consent to perform the ceremony. The entire day passed without me making the call. Late on the second day, I finally placed it. The message I delivered was not the one agreed upon with my kitchen table advisors. I was quite anxious about what my bride's reaction to what I was doing would be. I risked his refusal by stating to him I could not make the promise he asked for but would promise to respond if God came and asked me personally. At the time, I argued my point on the merits of honesty and integrity, though at the time thinking I was faithfully defending my disbelief in God.

When the conversation ended, the decision was made that the marriage could be performed in the church, whether in spite of my stand or because of it I was never sure. As I gloated after being given approval, I was aware of a discomforting feeling that something had started within me. Not knowing much about God, I managed to ignore it for a long time afterward.

The marriage survived and even prospered, with my wife proving to be the lifeline that kept me from being blown away by my own whirlwinds. I now realize that God has put my wife, who is one of the best things in my life, at my side. My introduction to her occurred in a way that defies circumstance and logic. My initial attraction to her never would have indicated that God was the source of this gift to my life. I have often abused this gift, yet like God she has never turned away from me.

My wife has never claimed any special awareness of God, though I think her survival through my lowest times has only been possible through the gifts God blessed her with and the presence of God's Spirit I have been able to feel through her. I am not sure how God would explain my presence in her life.

We continue to differ in many ways, yet we have witnessed the positive effects we have had on our children and the other people whose lives have touched our own. This girl who became my wife became the secure end of a lifeline for me. Without her, my loneliness and lack of love for the people around me would have eventually led to exile, perhaps even self-destruction. Our marriage ceremony, arrogantly negotiated, was performed in one of God's stone temples. Now here I stand, being built into a living temple. I didn't know it then, but God had already come to me by the time I had my awkward conversation with that minister.

Today's reading, from Corinthians, has shown me how the gifts we receive are meant for others. Not only can they be life-changing, but also life-supporting. I can see once again how generous God is in giving me life, abundant life. God knew what my needs would be long before I did and provided for me, but I missed seeing it because of my pride, disbelief and self-focus.

I spent years building a private cell, feeling unlovable and not knowing how to love. I did not believe such a love existed as what God has given me through her. This meant that I could not fully receive love, and certainly I could not give it—even to myself.

Seeing God's presence in my wife and in the use of her gifts helps me to look for my own gifts and determine to put them to good use.

Loving and knowing you are loved are desirable tenants in the Boarding House.

Coach's Corner
staying on track

ven after all this time and having benefited so much, I was tempted to skip my time with the boarder to gain a few precious minutes in today's schedule. Fortunately the warnings came back to mind and I didn't. In today's reading, Paul writes to the Christians in Thessalonica. The tone of this letter reminds me of a basketball coach preparing his players for a big game. Like a coach, he says these words to them: *"Stand firm and keep a strong grip on everything we taught you..."* (2 Thessalonians 2:15)

These are the exact words of encouragement I need to hear today.

The past couple of weeks have been quite hectic. It has required a great deal of determination to set aside time to pray and read a few verses. It is still tempting when things are busy to postpone my time with God instead of making the rest of my schedule wait. Even as I pick up the Bible today, I have a prickling awareness of the fast current of demands that are trying to pull me from my resolve to step into this time frame.

Paul and his team would probably understand the pressure I'm feeling right now. Not only that, but through these words I think I'm starting to understand theirs.

I don't mean that the exact circumstances exist for us both, more than two thousand years apart, but these people, too, must have faced interference from obstacles and temptations which prevented them from enjoying and benefiting from having a daily conversation with God. Knowing this helps me to resist the deceitful, worrying thoughts about the consequences of putting off my business responsibilities or the mocking question of what difference it makes if I take the time to read a few verses or not.

Shouldn't I have a stronger resolve by now? Where do these fears and doubts come from? One source is probably my awareness of all the things I have done wrong in my life, including the little things I continue to mess up each day. These thoughts stir up feelings of shame and embarrassment, easily pushing me into a negative attitude. Nothing seems right when I feel this way. I am assailed by feelings of unworthiness, especially when it comes to God's time.

The writers of the Bible warn me that there is usually something waiting to snatch the assurance and hope I receive from the Spirit out of my grasp. It is Satan, the spiritual being who twists everything he can into opposition to Jesus Christ. Like an opponent from the other team, his job is to keep me from scoring. Doubt, guilt, pride, and ignorance are the tools he utilizes to generate conflict within us in our daily decision-making.

The ongoing war between good and evil is often waged in the common circumstances of daily living where we are rushed, unsuspecting and pressured by how we want others to perceive us. Our daily encounters with people and circumstances include moments of choice and decision. Busyness, a general atmosphere of permissiveness, and a heightened sense of personal comfort and safety dull our definition of "right," "wrong," and "responsibility" at these times, making us vulnerable to temptation. When bad things happen, we tend to assume that it is just "part of life" or "punishment from God." These assumptions can camouflage Satan's objective to obstruct our relationship with God.

The Bible highlights the importance of developing a healthy, wholesome relationship with our Creator. It warns in many places of the serious interference of evil that Satan will direct at the world in general, and into our lives specifically. The activity of Satan corrupts love, justice, and authority in the world through the hearts and minds of individuals.

Satan lives in opposition to God, but in a spiritual dimension as does the Holy Spirit. Hearts and minds that have not been committed to faith in God are easy prey for this marauder.

Why does it have to be this way?

According to the Bible, the answer is the very essence of faith and free will. God will not force us into good behaviour. We choose whether or not we want God's Holy Spirit dwelling in us and leading our lives in that direction.

The process of making the choice strengthens us intellectually and spiritually, sharpening our sense of aliveness each day. The luxury of choice is probably one of God's most precious gifts, though at times like this I realize how I have ignored and abused it.

Many times, I wish God would just stop me in my thoughts or actions. I have often been angry because he didn't. Sometimes I even blame God for what I've done, because when I wasn't stopped I assumed my thoughts or actions were okay. Looking at it from the other side, though, I also know how indignant I would have been had God actually stepped in and controlled my behaviour.

Without this freedom to make wrong choices, I will never develop any sense of responsibility and accountability, nor will I ever feel the need to build a relationship with God. Free will was an expensive gift for God to give us, for Jesus had to die because of the way we use it. His death made it possible for people like me, who have not always made the right choices, to be saved from the ultimate penalty for those wrong choices. We may condemn each other for them but we are not condemned by God!

People who do not know or accept that there is a vital choice to be made are vulnerable to the predatory evil set loose by Satan. Unfortunately, the work of Satan isn't quite as obvious or ominous in its appearance in life as it is in a Stephen King horror story. It's usually subtly disguised as something benign or acceptable. It can come in the guise of a frustrating but innocent schedule so full that I feel I don't have time for God.

My thoughts slip back to a basketball game and its fast, noisy pace as the ball flies and bounces from player to player charging to the net. Then, in the stillness as a shot is made, everyone breathlessly watches the ball's descent towards the hoop. Once the ball hits the backboard, the commotion resumes until the next shot. Focusing on this start and stop action, my routine of prayer and Bible reading feels similar to this game's tempo. This prompts me to flip backwards through the pages of my prayer journals, taking note of the date preceding each entry. There are missing dates, marking the days where I chose to yield to my immediate schedule.

I read several of those entries following a period of absence from this prayer time. Invariably they start with an acknowledgement that I am feeling estranged from the calm confidence and safety I always find in my prayer times with God.

Paul's advice to this congregation is to resolve to hold onto the truth. That he gives this advice indicates that there are forces of logic, pride, and convenience that will snatch God's message away from us if we fail to secure it in our hearts and minds. I doubt Paul ever actually shot hoops, but if he had, he might have used a basketball game as an analogy for his teaching to this group of people. In the game, only the players who listen to the coach and develop the correct skills are able to manoeuvre the ball through the obstacles to "sink the hoop." Learning to live in God's Word is the same.

Simply knowing about God will not give me or anyone else a strong enough hold on the "ball." I need to understand and believe the message in a way that secures it in my heart, so that I will not be easily distracted or discouraged when faced with a challenge. Whether learning how to be a winning basketball player or a person living a hope- and love-filled life, it is crucial to listen and practice what the coach teaches.

I will always be prepared and able to do my best in those moments of confrontation if I "take five" with the Coach every day.

No Sweat

anything is possible

Mark 6:30–44

A common phrase comes to mind as I read these verses from the book of Mark—"No sweat." It's a flippant expression of confidence and exuberance in the face of a difficult, if not impossible, challenge. "No sweat" probably has a counterpart in every language.

There are two places in this passage where I can imagine hearing this phrase. The first time is at the beginning, when the disciples return in twos from the trips Jesus sent them on to neighbouring towns. In marked contrast to the first time he sent them out, this time they return with news of success. It's easy to picture their faces and feel their pride and confidence as they report to Jesus. They have each come a long way since the day Jesus asked them to join him. At that time every one of those disciples was carrying the weight of personal doubt, fears, and temptations. Maybe, like me, they were also even dealing with broken relationships or past sins.

Now, their faith and acceptance of what Jesus taught them has not only renewed them, but enabled them to deliver renewal of heart, mind, and body to others around them.

So I expect they were exuding a very positive attitude as they reported to Jesus, interrupting each other as they excitedly recounted stories of success. It's easy for me to hear them exclaim, "No sweat," in a self-congratulatory manner, as they let Jesus know they are ready and willing to accept their next assignment.

According to this account, their next opportunity for service was close at hand, only this time, Jesus is the one saying, "No sweat."

When Jesus directed his disciples to feed the five thousand, they must have been incredulous. After all, this occurred well before franchise restaurants were on every corner offering takeout service. Even if such restaurants *had* existed, they would have been beyond the disciples' financial capabilities. But this didn't affect Jesus' expectation that they were able to do what he had asked of them. Like a good and patient teacher, he allowed them time to search their own knowledge base first. Once they had considered the situation and came to the conclusion that it couldn't be done, he proceeded to demonstrate instant catering in a time of need.

First, he asked that they bring to him whatever food was available. When the inadequate loaves of bread and fishes were placed before him, he must have smiled confidently at the expressions of doubt on their faces.

He had seen that look before.

After accepting the meagre offerings, I can hear him say, "No sweat," as he directed his disciples to ready the crowd for their meal. As though to ensure that no one would miss the point of what had taken place here, there is more food remaining after everyone eats than was originally available.

This is a fascinating story, but what is its point? Does it mean we never have to buy food again? As appealing as the possibility sounds, it is also ridiculous.

I think Jesus performed this miracle for two reasons. The first is simply to demonstrate that he can and will provide for even our most basic needs. The second is to impress on his disciples that there are no limits to what is possible for them to accomplish through faith in God. During his thirty years on earth, Jesus frequently demonstrated astounding examples of the capabilities of faith. He also understands how difficult our logic makes it for us to believe in miracles, or that he is the son of God.

In situation after situation, Jesus demonstrated that he was capable of feats we consider to be impossible. In almost every one of those instances, he either did or said something to demonstrate that his accomplishment was not important by itself. Each was done to give proof of God's existence, power, compassion, and love to our doubting minds. Apparently the disciples needed these confirmations as much as I do.

Interestingly, it is easy for me to identify with Jesus in this story. As the story opens, he had obviously been working very hard for a long stretch of time. He needed a break, as did the disciples. I know what it feels like to be so tired that I just want everything to stop so I can get some rest. I don't want to listen to another word from anyone. I don't care if someone needs something from me. I just want a break from it all. Yet when he was faced with all these people, Jesus took the time to notice their needs and decided to look after them before himself. He wanted the disciples to do the same.

He responded to those people who had come to him believing in his capabilities, and perhaps even his identity. Not only did he provide teaching for their spiritual hunger, but also food for their physical needs. Providing far more than we could ever ask or imagine seems to me to be a recurring theme of Jesus' work and ministry.

Though he is always encouraging spiritual knowledge, growth, and obedience to God's laws and will, he is also full of compassionate answers to our physical needs. This is not the action of a selfish deity who seeks to control and restrain our lives. The message I get from these stories—and as the changes in my life convincingly prove to me—is that God cares about the wholeness of my existence and loves me in a way that is unique from all other forms and definitions of love I have ever seen or heard about. This love has an honesty and perfection to it that goes far beyond the very best love offered by parents, siblings, friends, or lovers. God wants us to know that his love is safe, complete, and can be trusted implicitly. His love will not mire us in the disappointment contained in the love offered by an unbelieving world.

I think of the huge amounts of time I expend in worry and effort to provide all the necessities of life in the twenty-first century—housing, food, education, retirement, and all the other concerns involving the well-being of my family. Jesus acknowledges the importance of these things, but he pushes me to understand that there is more to life than this immediacy to provide and survive. It doesn't take long to bring to mind the problems created by my concerted efforts to provide according to society's standards. Over time, this had led to anxiety and fear, as I realized my inability to protect and provide for myself or my family against everything that this world could pit against me.

I recall another story where Jesus matter-of-factly provided in abundance. It followed an all-night fishing trip by some of his disciples who were commercial fishermen by trade. They depended on fishing for their livelihood and knew how to fish, yet conditions were such that they returned empty-handed. Understanding their need, he instructed them to dip their net once more—it resurfaced full of fish. He will do the same for me.

Filling an empty net or feeding a huge crowd under impossible circumstances shows how Jesus recognizes our needs and is willing to answer them. He will provide all we need and sometimes more, though that may be different from all we want. He wants us to shift our primary focus from our material concerns to trust and hope in his presence and direction, preparing for the destination beyond this life, which most of us view very casually, if at all. Like all journeys, the route we take and our responses to events along the way determine whether the right destination is reached.

Once Jesus departed from his physical human form here on earth, his work continued through the Holy Spirit's working in individual men and women who believed, just as those disciples eventually did. This explains those earlier Bible readings which state that each person needs to be rebuilt as a temple or dwelling place for the Holy Spirit. This is why the Spirit of God is present to work and serve.

Each man and woman who steps out in belief and accepts the Holy Spirit will have their physical and spiritual needs met, and will in turn be able to give to others as Jesus gave to them. It sounds like an irresponsible, if not impossible, approach to life, but the examination and testing of God's Word proves that it works. The only point about it that can be dangerous is that we may exercise free will. The Spirit does not control or force us to think in a certain way—and I know that I don't always make the right choices. I can accept or ignore the prodding of the Spirit, but I will never be forced to go in a particular direction without my permission. Thankfully, though, neither will I ever be abandoned if I make the wrong choices. Jesus made sure I can have a way back.

Reading the books of the New Testament and seeking an understanding of them through prayer enables me to follow the accomplishments of those first disciples and the successes of the people who responded to them. There have been many books published through the years that bear witness to how this response in faith has continued through the lives of many people since that time, just as Jesus promised. Wherever a person has offered the faith and obedience God calls for, Jesus has delivered—no sweat.

I think of my own tremulous steps forward and the fantastic results I have experienced since doing so. Those disciples could not possibly have been any more awestruck by the feeding of the five thousand than I am by the new life I'm now living. I would never have believed that the mess I was in could ever be fixed—by anyone.

There are lots of people who want a new beginning, like I did. I now know what Jesus' response will be to all who ask.

"No sweat."

Sandbags

protection and assurance

T here is one thing I know for sure as I sit here this morning. Something has changed. Me. I'm not the same person I was sixty-four days ago.

I remember my first encounter with Jesus and marvel at how different I feel now. Before his arrival in my life, I was desperately lost amidst what I described as the Mad Parade. I was confused, frightened, angry, lonely in the crowd and lacking hope that it could be any other way. I had been defeated by what I saw as my inability to understand the madness in the world around me or the doubt and storm within myself.

Recently, television reports have again displayed video coverage of devastating floods in various places around the world. Unrelenting rains and runoff water choke riverbeds and then rampage over the banks, destroying homes, stealing fertile soil, burying streets with mud and washing away roads. Some communities feverishly build sandbag dykes along the riverbanks to deflect the attack. Those that aren't prepared must evacuate and watch the rising water sweep through the doors and windows of the unprepared homes according to its destructive whims—or drown.

While watching, the thought occurred to me that I was like one of those houses as I helplessly watched the Mad Parade overtake me. The problems I was experiencing due to my lack of preparation and attitude were like floodwaters pushing through every chink and crack of my inadequate defences. I had no wall

Greg R. Elliott

of sandbags around me. The flood was about to swallow me just as I was hoisted from a spiritual drowning by Jesus.

These words paint a dramatic scene, but they don't exaggerate the threat I was feeling. Physically, at the time, I lived my life each day trying to function and perform to the few positive standards I had been able to distinguish. Internally, or spiritually, the swirling chaos kept me in suspended fear, eroding everything it touched.

Jesus rescued me from this mental drowning. It could have led, as it has for others, to a breakdown or destructive behaviour, even physical death. It was a horrible time and only now, safely removed from it, am I able to view it with confidence rather than fear.

What changed? Not the flood or the world around me.

What needed to change? Certainly the world does, but that is not the starting point. I needed to change first. I certainly wanted to change and have a new life—however, I did not see believing in God, reading the Bible and praying regularly as the answer. But I was in danger and needed to be rescued. That is what Christ did for me. Like one of those helicopters in the videos that lift the people stranded in trees and on rooftops, he rescued me.

It took a while for my resistance to let go and accept his rescue and believe that his offer of love and restoration was real. Next came my embarrassment because of my previous rejection of him. This was followed by my awareness and shame about some of the things I had done in my life.

Reading the Bible quickly laid all of this aside though, quelling my fear that it would make me ineligible for the new life I needed.

In these verses today, Paul's words draw the whole thing together for me again, giving me a great feeling of comfort and thankfulness. This new perspective on who I can become, combined with the confidence of knowing there is a loving Creator who cares for me, makes it possible for me to learn a lesson from the flood metaphor. The flood that life situations and circumstances can bring is much bigger than me and I cannot stand against it and survive on my own.

I now realize my stubborn insistence on "doing it my way" kept me in ignorance of God's existence and the fullness of life available through faith in him. If life, and the challenges and hardships it sometimes brings, can be compared to a river that floods on occasion, we need to be prepared. God's Word provides the fill for those sandbags that will protect us in the difficult times that threaten our wholeness. If we fail to have those sandbags ready, we will need to be rescued from the flood.

196

I am inadequately prepared to handle all the storms and trials life can bring. My anger, fear, and confusion have been fuelled by my misguided pride and lack of faith. I am not alone. I do not need to feel alone. Christ is patient, vigilant, and ready to help the moment I reach out, in spite of the multitude of times I have ignored his presence.

These are powerful, life-building truths to uncover; they release tears of shame, followed by tears of gratitude. Only love has such authority.

My thoughts return to the example of the flood and dykes.

I now feel a confidence and have insight that I never had before. There is no guarantee against future floods but there is a way to be prepared and a guarantee of rescue if required.

I just need to keep the sandbags filled.

Redesignation
no longer the same

EPHESIANS 6:18–20, JOHN 3:1–3

provide a stark comparison with the situation Paul is writing from in Ephesians 6. He is in prison because he believes in God. I was locked in a cell because I did not.

Paul's jailers were motivated by jealousy, anger, and perhaps even fear. Those same elements were present in my captivity, the difference being that the jealousy, anger, and fear were within me; therefore, I was in the unique position of being both the prisoner and the jailer. Paul and I were each imprisoned because of our actions but what a difference between his and mine.

In this letter to his friends and church members, Paul directs them to continue praying for themselves and all others so that they will be open to receive whatever direction God's Spirit may give them. He also asks them to pray for him so that he will be able to do an even better job of what got him thrown into jail—sharing what he knows about Jesus. His faith and courage fill me with admiration, though I now understand how his faith and the Holy Spirit were amplifying Paul and his capabilities in this way.

I sent no such letters from my cell and had no courage of faith and commitment. The only things I might have metaphorically authored during my imprisonment would be letters of complaint and blame. My concerns never extended to having hope for myself let alone anyone else.

There are so many differences between Paul and me as I look at our jail cell stories. This was not always the case, however, because Paul was once also in the same kind of self-constructed cell from which I have just escaped. His story is more dramatic than mine, though we each benefited from the same escape plan.

Jesus made himself known to us both and then introduced his Holy Spirit into the mix, who was tasked with introducing us to ourselves. This off-the-wall task was accomplished through the equally odd method of pointing us back to Jesus and God, giving us the opportunity to study and understand who they are and what they are doing. As this took place, we found that the heavy tarps keeping our reality hidden from our self-perception were being folded back. We were able to see what God saw in us. It wasn't a very flattering sight. This new awareness of ourselves, combined with the knowledge the Spirit gave us of Jesus' teaching, kick-started us both into the necessary mode of wanting to change ourselves because we were also shown what we could be.

The conversation between Nicodemus and Jesus, recounted in John 3, describes again, using another metaphor, the vital doorway Paul and every person who wants new life must step through.

My thoughts return to the original house image in the form of a "before" photo if on a television house reno show. I notice something that I missed on my last visit. The windows are strongly girded with iron bar shutters and complicated locks. They are intimidating, and only the most foolish or determined could miss or ignore their purpose. A closer examination of those shutters, however, reveals an interesting uniqueness about them. They are installed backwards. Rather than simply protecting from unwanted outside entry, they also prevented exit from the inside.

While the finely wrought iron finials on the rooftop indicate that the house was intended to be a fine stately home, this metalwork contrarily declares it to be some odd kind of prison.

I think for a moment about what has taken place since the arrival of the Holy Spirit. The first step evicted the most undesirable tenants and put other rowdy ones on notice. The step-by-step cleaning gradually created open space and the clean air of freshness allowing for freer passage and increased comfort. Dangerous, useless or spoiled articles are gone and the task of sorting and categorizing the much-reduced but remaining boxes and piles of stuff is getting easier. Abused or neglected elements that were once valuable are restored to their full usefulness.

The renovation involved opening spaces up, bringing in more light, and providing better support for the service and maintenance of the house. Access to the house has been improved. As each aspect of the process is undertaken and completed, another is identified. Enthusiasm for the job continues to heighten, reenergizing those periods when the work is difficult or slower.

Until seeing those inside-out bars and locks, I was ready to declare with pride that the project was complete. This latest finding indicates that a consultation with the project manager is in order, so I promptly clear the worktable and invite the boarder to another on-site meeting.

These meetings, in prayer, are a welcome feature of the project and a vital part of my routine. Our conversations usually start with questions from me and wrap up with satisfying, though often surprising, answers. This one is no exception. I pose my questions. I think I understand the unusual number of locks on the doors of my house, but why are the bars and locks also on the windows? What is the significance of discovering these locks immediately after reading the scene between Jesus and Nicodemus?

In response, my mind is nudged through the three verses of John's recording again. It appears Nicodemus fully believes that Jesus is who he claims to be. He acknowledges his acceptance of the miracles Jesus performs as proof of his having a direct connection with God. Elsewhere, Nicodemus is recorded as holding an important senior teaching position in the temple, so this confession of belief separates him from his peers in their refuting of Jesus. Such a confession, if widely known, would have jeopardized his honoured standing in the religious establishment of the day and altered, if not ended, his leadership role.

My expectation is that this admission would please Jesus. Instead, Jesus appears to ignore these signs of a good follower and replies, *"I assure you, unless you are born again, you can never see the Kingdom of God"* (John 3:3). Huh?

The mental nudge of the project manager has to become a strong push before the meaning of this statement takes shape. When Jesus used the words "born again," he obviously intended an entirely new heart and way of thinking—not just a convenient, comfortable adjustment.

The clean up of the Boarding House has rid the house of the major problem tenants and replaced the agitation with calmness, while the restoration and renovation are returning purpose and beauty to the structure. I believe in God. I accept what Jesus has given me as a model of character. I have examined my attitudes and made some serious adjustments. I have released my grip on old memories of anger and jealousy. I now recognize destructive patterns of thought and behaviour and avoid them. I have forgiven and been forgiven. Is there something else yet?

My question reveals an attitude that God wants me to examine, which is why the image of the iron bars still shielding the windows of this wonderful new house has been pointed out to me.

I was willing to think the renovation was done. All that was left was to enjoy what I had accomplished and acquired through this supernatural construction team. But it seems there is more to it. This is the beginning. Continued maintenance will be required. No doubt I have kept a few things tucked away because they were favourite possessions, or were so familiar that I deemed them necessary. They will warrant further scrutiny and evaluation. The Boarding House is to be the place in which I live and grow and welcome others. It will be a safe and nurturing haven from which I can go out into the world, confidently and creatively.

The renovation has further potential beyond healing me and providing me with a safe and comfortable home. There are other people who live in the misery of spiritual and physical prisons. Like the men and women who lived with Jesus and were asked to share what they learned from him, I can now use my freedom to share what I have learned so far.

I think that the iron shutters indicate that I am holding back, not really trusting myself yet or confident that I am a new person—afraid that other people won't accept me as a new person. Once again, the words in the Bible have shown me something I would not otherwise see.

This house is no longer designated for demolition. It is no longer a prison either. It is now the healthy restored home of my new life.

I am no longer a prisoner!

It's time to throw those shutters into the dumpster too.

Safety Zone
looking back

ACTS 1:6–9

N ovels and movies often open the depiction of wartime conflict with a narration from a setting safely removed from the actual battle but within earshot of the action. These accounts evoke heavy emotion and a sense of drama through juxtaposing the sounds of the conflict as they rumble across the land and through the darkness of night with the safer setting of the narrator. This perspective provides an opportunity for one of the characters in the story to provide a commentary on the distant rumblings, interrupted occasionally by the visual punctuation of explosions and fires flashing in the night skies. There is an uncomfortable mixed sense of both threat and safety.

This could describe my current sense of being in a similar manner. I feel like I could be pictured sitting on the front porch of the Boarding House on a quiet summer night, calm and safe, though aware of the rumble of discord and conflict in the distance. I know what it is.

In today's reading from Acts it is easy for me to think that the disciples were in a similar frame of mind. After nearly three years with Jesus, they continue to ask questions that show they are not completely sure what Jesus is doing or what they are to do now. Like me, they appear to be straddling their hope, that Jesus is finally about to radically change the problems of the world around them, and their worry, about their role and well-being in it if he doesn't. To their question, Jesus appears almost dismissive as he tells them that they don't need to know the details. Then, after a quick reminder of the impending arrival of God's Spirit and telling them to get on with the job given to them of witnessing to the world about him and what he has done—he disappears.

I feel somewhat open-mouthed, as I'm sure they did, by the shortness of his response. It feels like there are a lot of blanks to fill in and more questions to be answered yet. But there is no time for discussion. His departure leaves no option other than to think about what they have seen and learned as they await the Spirit.

I decide to do the same and through a short prayer, somewhat hesitantly, ask the Spirit to accompany me on a virtual visit back to the source of the distant rumble—the Mad Parade.

An involuntary wince pulls my muscles tight as the image reappears. Nothing has changed, it is still clamour and confusion. First, I relive the body-slamming punch of emotional panic while shuffling along deep within the crowded, rabble-rousing dysfunction of the parade. Next I relive the hopelessness while sitting on the curb, exhausted after struggling out of its aimless animation and realizing I would soon be snatched back into it. The visit lasts only moments and then—like Jesus in this reading—it evaporates.

Though I am able to empathize deeply with its hostages, I realize I am no longer subject to the parade's spiritual and emotional abuse. Instead, I have been shown how to stay out of it. I am filled with confidence, hope and thanksgiving; this brief visit to where I once was gives me an understanding into what Jesus is saying to that small group of people—and across time—to me.

Though we were given free will to make our own choices in life, the Mad Parade is not God's Parade. It is not what God intended for us. It is the result of our rejection of God, either intentionally, through neglect or through never being told God was there.

Looking around the world, my neighbourhood, my family, myself—it is easy to see what happens when people exercise their free will without the benefit of understanding God's guidelines on how to use it safely and productively. I can see how people who live and act solely from their selfishly directed free will can do tremendous damage—emotionally, physically and spiritually—not only to themselves but to the people around them. The Bible is very clear that is not what God intended.

Prior to meeting the Holy Spirit I thought the Mad Parade was just rotten luck in my life and everybody else lived the good life. Now I can see it has always existed and many people have been deceived and trapped by its shiny appearance and hollow promises.

Ultimately the future of our unfolding world is in God's hands but our use of free will can make the present miserable and the future look grim. However, those who are given new understanding and hope for the future from God—new life—rebirth—are now able to share God's hope for us and encourage other people who face trouble or defeat in their lives. The Bible tells us that Jesus came so that we could live life and live it abundantly—not marching as a captive in the Mad Parade. That is what his friends standing there with him in his last moments on earth were asked to tell the world.

The story of how they and others did that eventually ended up in my paperback Bible and lets me and everyone else who reads the Bible know that we don't have to live in the rumble, conflict and pain of the Mad Parade.

Like those first men and women who knew Jesus personally, we can tell doubting, hurting people that there is a Parade of Hope and a place for them in it—it is well described in the New Testament.

The Throne Room

looking forward

REVELATION 7:9–17, JOHN 14:16–17

There was a point in time when I wondered whether I could or would carry on living. I also had a very brief but desperate period when I considered whether another human being should continue living. Fortunately both times were passed through.

The renovation of my heart and mind has changed much within me, resulting in an entirely new way in how I live my life. I am happy with what has happened. In the process of the renovation though, I learned that there is not only this life to be lived but another after it. My logic, which has proven to be inadequate or wrong many times now, has no explanation for me as to how this is possible.

Even popular culture tells us where this next life is to be lived—either in Heaven or Hell—but they are spoken of more as a joke than a reality

Though the Bible does mention them, thus far, neither of these places has been the subject of my daily routine and in a way I almost feel silly mentioning them. Nonetheless, I have become convinced of the existence of something else for us after our life here on earth. What that life will be like, I do not know. To my surprise, instead of wanting to shrug this concept off as a bit of science fiction, it has given me a tremendously positive attitude. I want to understand more about the implications of such a reality even though I may be inviting a challenge that will be answered in uncomfortable ways.

The reading I'm given for today's foray into prayer is from the very last book of the Bible—Revelation. My knowledge about this book is sketchy, though I do realize it is supposed to have been written by one of the original disciples of Jesus, a man named John. It's a record of a series of visions, or revelations, that were given to him during a very difficult time for the early Christians. He was to relay the information in these visions to specific fledgling churches so that they would learn what God wanted them to know. The events described, and creatures envisioned, are quite unfamiliar in this current age, unless we encounter them in sci-fi or vampire movie scenes.

In the timeframe of this writing, I assume most people were better able to interpret the meaning of the images than I am, here in the twenty-first century. My lack of knowledge about these elements of the text probably impede comprehension, so I'm not really convinced there's much point in reading these words. In spite of that reservation, I carry on, having learned the profit in doing so.

When I finish reading these few verses, I feel disappointed, if not offended. This scene contradicts the image I have built of Jesus as an in-the-street activist. Instead it reminds me of old movies depicting pagans at worship. This excerpt from Revelation depicts a personality quite opposite to the Jesus who pushed me out of the Mad Parade and later opened my cell door. It is certainly not the image given of Jesus in the other books of the Bible. I don't like the idea of an enthroned Jesus as the Christ letting people fall at his feet like this. Have I been misled, or is something missing here?

I mentally picture the scene as John describes it. There is an enormous crowd of people, representative of all human races, a throne, angels, and creatures such as those described in books of Greek mythology. My imagination completes the image with glistening marble flooring in an open plaza, a warm sun above, a lush flower garden with white walls and columns of carved stone framed by a Mediterranean blue sky. Overall, it has the appearance of a living tableau arranged by Dali, the twentieth century surrealist artist known for his often puzzling paintings. The setting itself appears inviting, but I'm still not at all comfortable with Jesus being enthroned this way. Nothing I have experienced so far has indicated he would be like this. If this is representative of life in Heaven, I'm not so sure it is going to entice and fill me with hope for very long. What message can there be in this?

I read a little further. One of the leaders approaches John and asks him a question. John's response enables me to realize that he doesn't have any better grasp on the meaning of this diorama than I do. This encourages me. For the moment, we have something in common. The man continues and, though no explanation is given of the setting, one is given about the actions of the people in it. These people are expressing their gratefulness for the forgiveness and new life they have received from God, in whose presence they now live. That at least I can identify with.

I sit for a little while after completing the reading. Puzzlement and a whisper of dissatisfaction still hover over my thoughts like a mist. I don't want to think that this is what Heaven is like. I finally ask my boarder for help. Several minutes of quiet contemplation follow, eventually bringing a gentle laugh to my mind and lips.

Maybe John and I have something else in common. I'm certainly not a disciple like him, nor have I been entrusted with messages from the future. I have, however, been treated to images of things to help me understand myself and the Bible and recognize God's involvement in my life—the Mad Parade, Zacchaeus on the limb, the Boarding House and the shepherds on the hill. None of these metaphors was to be interpreted as absolute literal truth. They are montages assembled with various visual elements I will recognize. Each presented a difficult concept to grasp in a visual story, providing me with easier access to understanding. It amuses me to think of this great disciple sitting with me in a large-screen theatre, being treated to such a unique process of explanation and discovery.

Now, again, God's Spirit pushes me past the limitation of my logic which keeps me from understanding anything beyond the literal or familiar. I remember a Bible reading several weeks ago which left me feeling so incredibly aware of God's love and care for me that I sat in my office chair and cried. I had never felt such sheer joy before. After several minutes of tears, I got out of the chair and knelt on the floor, bumbling out "Thank you" in a repetitive string. This soon led to me doing a happy dance, laughing and crying simultaneously. When it finally ran out, I laughed at what my childish display of joy must have looked like. Since then, I've heard a contemporary hymn, *Lord of the Dance* written by Sidney Carter, which has in its chorus the words, "Dance then wherever you may be", which reminds me of that day and renews the enjoyment of it every time I hear it.

I try to remember what specific occurrence took place to warrant such an outburst of joy that day and unbelievable as it sounds, I can't. How can I have been so happy and thankful and not be able to remember anything more than that it came in response to realizing God loves me?

Thoughts of the crowd in the story return to me. John's writing explains that they are in the company of Jesus, having left this world and life. There was no mention of flames so they must then be in Heaven. They have completed the journey I am in the midst of today. Those people endured sickness, pain, fear, loss, and a multitude of other struggles and broken dreams, and now they are in a place where no such trials exist. What an exhilarating experience that would be!

I now realize that the literal setting of John's vision is not the object of the teaching. The setting is merely the method God used to help John grasp the depth of joy faithful people would find upon arriving in Heaven. It would be so great as to defy description, yet God wants those of us who read this to at least glimpse enough of it to strengthen and encourage us as we battle our own shadows, survive the difficult times and face the unknown in our journey towards this destination.

Viewed from this perspective, instead of taking offence at what I interpreted as blind, robotic submission, I now empathize with the endlessness of their thanksgiving and their joyous simplicity in expressing it. Their actions prove that Jesus shared himself with and for each of them in the same powerful and personal way he has with me. John's writing lets me know that Jesus came to him, too, in a unique, personal, and convicting manner.

I first knew Jesus as a rescuer as I huddled and shook in my weary uncertainty. Then I met him in the Holy Spirit, as a friend, guide and healer, sitting on a faded worn chair in the Boarding House rather than on a majestic throne. He is always serving *me*. Never has there been any hint that he expects me to fall prone before him.

The Bible claims that he will do this for every person who invites him into his or her life. Obviously, John's vision testifies to his having done so for a multitude of people. But even seated on this regal throne, the vision describes him as a lamb, not a ruler.

As I lean back and think about today's time in prayer and reading, I am struck once again by the contrast between my first reading of these verses and the one guided by my teacher, the Holy Spirit. I read the same words each time, but on the first reading I missed the richness of its meaning by relying on my own near-sighted logic.

I go on now to the second reading listed in the guidebook, another written by John. It is short but opens another door to deep understanding.

My thoughts are returned to the people who were described as bowing and singing their thankfulness. Maybe they went through a renovation of heart and mind like I am doing. Maybe they too once lived two lives—one on the exterior, which everyone saw and recognized as normal, while the other, where uncertainty and harshness reigned, was hidden.

Like me too, they probably encountered days or circumstances that rekindled old habits or doubts from the "me I no longer want to be". I'm confused about my inclination to still occasionally act and think in this manner. My expectation was that all these old ways would change totally and immediately once I finally invited Jesus into the clutter of my life. I get disappointed when these moments return, even though the Holy Spirit is now with me. How was that possible? At those times, I fear that the Spirit will leave me again.

With this reading from John 14 God again assures me that the Spirit is not a fickle tenant about to rent a moving van and seek better accommodations. The Spirit's purpose is to help me know the truth about God. This will be a lifelong friendship, regardless of the challenges I will undoubtedly provide.

The people gathered in the diorama John describes have gone through all this as well and yet they stayed the course, as did the Spirit. The Spirit will also help me over the slips I will still make—guiding me, correcting me, protecting me, helping me understand God's will for me—whether I'm struggling some days or happy dancing with gratitude—wherever I may be.

The New Me
new life, new possibilities

The day is beginning with a buzz and a real desire to get into my Bible reading time. What a change this is from the earlier, tight chest days that insisted my schedule was far too busy to consider spending time in prayer.

What a contrast this is to the dread that greeted me each day when I was a marcher in the Mad Parade. Much to my surprise, the book I had been so dismissive of proved to be the route to what I was so desperately looking for. Though initially I was reluctant to enter this experience, it eventually silenced the reveille of cold fear that ended my nights and gruffly introduced another day while extinguishing the flaming anger that fuelled my charge through life. I wasn't exactly sure who I was in those days, but usually my self-perception cast me as the scruffy underdog that no one, including me, thought could ever be anything else. My defence was to hide behind the maximum-security walls of resistance I had built.

My approach to life had been similar to Zacchaeus, a businessman in one of those Bible stories. I thought I could do life my own way and watch the happenings from a secluded perspective, without involvement, thinking no one cared about or noticed me. I observed people and events through the squinted eyes and sceptical heart of a "Doubting Thomas," another person in those Bible stories who needed tangible proof before he could trust or believe anything.

Those days were without hope, but like in a good Disney movie, just at the right moment someone came along who was not driven away by my elevator moods and instead got into my isolated compound. Gentleness and love were the tools Jesus used for this break-in. He is the rescuer who showed me that I could be much more.

A day came when, having found no other solution to the agitation and uncertainty that filled my mind, I resigned myself to reading the Bible.

My caustic opinion of the Bible quickly proved to be the result of knowing so little about it. I found in it incredible encounters various individuals had with God. I found fascinating stories of sex, politics, adventure, and intrigue to rival any modern tabloid or insider television show. Some of those people wanted a new life too.

I learned that these words have been preserved, translated, retranslated, tested, retested, and lived out in both trial and celebration by many generations of people. In it were the stories of people who came to recognize the presence of a living Creator out in the desert, by a riverbank, on a battlefield, in a courtroom, in times of loss, in every cluttered corner of their minds, and in those raw, open spaces where there is no place to hide, where we can be seen for who and what we are. They had been people like me.

As I read the entries I have written following my prayer times, I can see how my life has changed. I can now say that I understand those words the apostle Paul wrote which puzzled me so much the first time I read them. I am one of those "temples" in which God's Spirit dwells.

It took a long time for me to accept this new identity, not believing that it was really possible for me. As I read from Colossians 3 today, I am able to understand and accept that Paul's salutation to those church members in the city of Colossae includes me. His speech is both an affirmation and a summary of what has taken place within me. In fact, these verses are like the congratulatory send-off given by a proud instructor to the successful graduates of a gruelling training program. This triumph bestows us with a new identity which we will honour and be recognized by.

Other than frowning less and smiling much more frequently, there is visibly little to indicate that anything is different about me, yet nothing is the same within me. Only my behaviour makes it apparent that I have new life and a new purpose. These verses heighten my awareness of the privilege and also the responsibility of this new identity and create a tingle like the nervous excitement experienced on the first day of a new job.

I recall a series of television commercials that aired a number of years ago for a highly respected global corporation. It was during the height of their prestige in the business world, when most new university graduates would consider a position with this company as their dream job. The commercials profiled a short line up of individuals whom the company had selected and prepared for their specific roles of representing this prestigious corporate giant. The effervescent pride these individuals displayed about their new identity was very apparent in those television spots. I'm sure that same pride would radiate from them every time they presented their business cards to future clients. Their business identity, and a significant portion of their personal identity, would be based on the reputation of excellence built and enjoyed by the company. These new recruits realized that the company's lofty profile was built upon the high standards set and lived by every individual member of its corporate family.

The commercials, however, did not show the countless hours of study and training these recruits had to invest to obtain their position. Nothing was shown of the pressure or failures along the route they had to face and conquer. We didn't see the landmark moments of growth and change that resulted in their success. That part of the story is contained within their hearts and memories, observable only in the integrity and compassion of how they do their work each day.

That is what Paul is writing about.

The inner calmness I now know, though not constant yet, is permanent. This core sense of peace and hope arrived the day I invited Jesus into my heart, described as the Boarding House. It is the result of the nourishing combination of insight, knowledge and understanding I've gained through the Holy Spirit and reading God's Word.

Even though the peace is itself a product of my process of change, it is also the processor through which I understand both the turmoil and source of my change. Peace comes from believing that God *is* and that Jesus is who he says he is. Such belief is what allowed those ten lepers that the writer Luke wrote about to be healed.

Those first twelve men who Jesus chose to accompany him came to absolute belief in Jesus' identity as the son of God. Paul came to the same understanding, and in turn it is what he introduced to other people—as Paul is doing in the letter I am reading today. This assurance is what I too will be able to share through the way I live my life.

Before the start of this renovation, or cleaning up of my act, I sporadically tried to improve my life by cutting out profane language, turning away from self indulgence, and giving up destructive habits. When this cleared my head somewhat but produced no evidence of God, I decided to study and apply myself more diligently, thinking I would then become a calmer, better person. It was frustrating to discover that this, too, failed to yield the full measure of what I sought. My next decision was to show up in church on Sunday mornings. I went on and on, checking items off my list as I tried to find God or earn God's approval. Each of these efforts brought about immediate benefits, but even all together they didn't make me feel complete.

Even after the reno started, I thought maybe I just needed to pray more. Maybe I was just not good enough and the ugly parts of my past really couldn't be forgiven. Maybe Jesus just didn't like me. Maybe he was only for people who knew everything about the church and God. I could fill pages with the negative thoughts about why I couldn't be one of God's people. The days when I felt this way were difficult, even fearful at times. God however, patiently put up with me and finally convinced me that I did belong.

Each of my doubts was heard and answered through the Spirit, and when I stopped doubting and squirming, the Spirit of God gave me a full conviction of God's acceptance of me. This went far beyond my expectations. Now I realize that God's acceptance is not a badge to be earned, but more like a gift that has to simply be accepted and unwrapped. The Holy Spirit's role is to accompany each man, woman, and child who has been born to recognize and find that treasure. For some people, it's a simple, short quest, while for others, like me, it is longer. The Bible makes it clear that God's intent and hope is that every one of us will complete the journey regardless of the route we take.

It's amazing for me to look back and see how it was my own reluctant will and logic, rather than my good or not-so-good deeds that delayed my breakthrough moment. My logic is itself a part of my creation, but like all other things, regardless of how good it is, it has limitations before God. Sidestepping my stubborn reliance on logic will allow me to step into the realm of faith. Like the people fishing that morning shortly after Christ's death, I've tried it my way. Do I now believe what God has taught me and trust his direction to try something else?

It looks as though it's time for me to dip my net on the other side of the boat, and expect it to be filled.

I chuckle as I picture myself in a line-up with smiling representatives of various successful corporations like Apple, Google, and Amazon—each of us confidently holding out our business cards with pride as we introduce ourselves and our new identities. Only mine isn't about selling a product or service—it's about showing people that an abundant new life is possible.

It's about letting people know that they don't have to feel lonely, angry or frightened. It's about letting a trapped person know there is a healthy way out. It's about comforting a hurting person, helping a neighbour find hope, sharing joy, offering directions to someone who is lost, letting others know they are valuable, there is forgiveness, purpose to life and someone who cares for them regardless of who they are or what they have done.

Yes, my card proclaims that I am one of God's children—free at last, and a "temple" for the Holy Spirit. I'm no longer the me I didn't want to be.

The apprentice has graduated. I'm a new guy, with a new life and new opportunities!

I think I will write another list, similar to the one I wrote some time ago that listed all the things I had done wrong in my life. This one though is going to be list all the things I am grateful for—all the things that have changed or are changing in my life—for the good. I think it is going to be a long list too.

Mirror, Mirror on the Wall
summing up the process and the results

ISAIAH 55

I sense this will be the last entry from my prayer journals, bringing my recording of the renovation of my heart and mind to a close—though a regular maintenance program is now in place and will continue.

The Spirit takes me back on two different pathways of thought today to reflect on all that has happened. First, I am returned to the Old Testament book titled Isaiah, which I have prayed through before. These repeat lessons have always brought fresh insights, and today is no exception.

The words printed here come from ancient times. In almost poetic terms, they present an unfamiliar setting for a twenty-first century reader. It would be easy to put this down and say that it has no relevance to me. I continue reading, though, because this text is the narrative of God speaking to the people of the time. I have learned that the meaning in such words is unconstrained by historical context. They contain wisdom for all people and times—including me and mine.

I am sometimes stumped by the complexities of daily life, whether from past times or current. There are also times when I am unable to grasp the relevance of the underlying meaning in the situations I read about. Not so when I'm with the Spirit. During my prayer times, my intellect and memory respond easily to the Spirit. My comprehension expands and absorbs, gently poking at my limited logic until understanding flows freely.

For instance, little time is required for me to understand the significance of the first verse in today's reading. I remember the hollow state of my life before meeting Jesus. I was unhappy, in spite of a freezer full of food, a house equipped with modern conveniences, and endless opportunities for parties, plays, and general self-indulgence. These are commonly accepted marks of success, so on the surface you could say that I was happy. But my unanswered pain, anger and doubt, buried deep within my self-awareness, fuelled my unhappiness. The surface happiness wasn't enough—and wasn't real.

Needless to say, my limited human logic tried to satisfy my yearning for more by acquiring more of anything and everything. It didn't fill the void. In fact if anything changed at all, it was the development of an even greater awareness of my undefined poverty. Thankfully, this bottomless pit has been filled since the new boarder's arrival.

As I write of this friend now, I return to the virtual Boarding House, the unique form of contact and teaching used by the Holy Spirit, whom I have come to know and trust. A bit of time has gone by since I last visited this fascinating diorama depicting my inner life.

Inside, walking along the main hallway towards the front door, my attention is caught by the shine of the natural wood flooring and the fresh whiteness of the woodwork and painted walls. Everything is so clean and new, including the gentle background sounds of activity elsewhere in the house. There is none of the clutter and disruptive noise that assaulted me on my first tour.

Light shines through the unshuttered panes of glass in the front door and dances across the surface of a mirror hanging on the wall. I don't remember seeing it before, but as I approach it I sense that the mirror is going to be the focus of my attention today. Looking into it, I see the same image I look at most days in my bathroom mirror. I was once able to look at myself in that bathroom mirror, but I started avoiding it when possible many years ago because the face looking back at me too often was tense and unhappy. The eyes always posed a question I didn't want to hear and couldn't answer. The simple solution was to not look at that face. The plea in my eyes also led me to avoid looking directly into the eyes of other people, because I did not want them to see what was there, either.

Today is different, though. I look at this reflection of myself in the Boarding House mirror and see softness and a smile that has never greeted me before. In my eyes, I see an inviting wholeness. As I study this new image, tears of gratitude form in my eyes.

A laugh skips out from me and fills the room. I'm reminded of the Queen in the old fairy tale who had a mirror into which she looked to have her questions answered. I jokingly wonder if my mirror could speak to me as well. Paraphrasing her famous line, I ask, "Mirror, mirror on the wall, who is this person looking back at me now?"

Fortunately there's no lightning bolt, menacing image, or thundering voice answering back, but the reflection does respond in the form of a series of smiling faces. The smiles in the mirror are from those men and women I have read about in the Bible. Probably because of my familiarity with the work of illustrators such as Rein Poortvliet or Richard Hook and painters like Michelangelo, the faces appear with the features given to them by these artists. Among them are Moses, David, Paul, Mary, Jonah, Lydia, Zacchaeus, and Thomas. One at a time, their familiar faces look back at me and hold my gaze. Each of them smiles in a way you would expect, based on their personality: Abraham as a wise and loving grandfather, Paul with understanding and sharp expectation, Mary rather shyly but with a challenging confidence, and Zacchaeus with the twinkle of fun and a knowing glow of shared adventure. I have enough time to think about each one of them and how reading their stories has affected me. As the reflection in the mirror becomes my own again, the thought strikes me that I am now, in a unique way, a reflection of them. I am what they were. Something common from their images has been passed on to me.

By that I do not mean to infer that I'm about to go and part a puddle, much less a sea, by waving my arms as Moses did. Nor am I about to defeat a giant warrior and become a ruling king, as David did. There's also no chance of me becoming the great missionary Paul was, traveling the continents with a message of new life. I don't expect to be swallowed by a whale like Jonah nor is my story likely to be included in a future edition of the Bible either.

What I have become and will be though, is a believer in and a child of the same God who loved each of them and whom they knew and loved. I belong to that same family of people in spite of the historical and cultural space between us. Every one of these men and women came to belief and trust in God. Because of that, they had an inner peace that enabled them to do some extraordinary things with their lives.

Some of them recognized and quickly responded to God. More than a few of them were like me and needed to be rescued before being able to recognize God and answer his call. Regardless of the difference in the way we met God, or what simple or stupendous results came from the meeting, I realize that I have something else in common with each of these individuals—their stories have been involved in my rescue and renewal.

The meaning of Paul's words about becoming a temple for God's Spirit became clear to me some time ago, and now his later words, about each of us being bricks assembled together into one temple for the Spirit, also assume clarity. God's one and only Spirit is the same builder of each of us, in both a direct personal manner and through each other. In a spiritual sense we are one, regardless of any geographic, generational, or other difference we have with one another. All who become dwelling places for God's Spirit become bricks in the all-inclusive temple of God's people. As such, the mirror's message to me is that we now share the same image.

A few moments pass while I marvel at my own reflection again. I'm smiling, and so are the other faces I have seen, but the experience we've all gone through has not simply been a "happy face" one. There was a time of passage but our lives have not been the same since encountering God and Jesus. None of us would want to return to what we were prior to our relationship with God.

Previously, I said that God gives this new life freely to all who ask. I pay nothing for the abundance I receive. God does not require payment for the freedom I have received since the arrival of the Spirit. My journal entries have inventoried the many insights and changes resulting in that freedom. The "cost" has come in the form of having to admit that I was wrong about so many things, that I hurt not only myself but many other people. My pride paid heavily for that realization. It was not easy to see myself as God could see me.

I experienced guilt and shame before I was able to turn them over to Jesus. It is awkward to realize that Jesus had to go through the humiliation and pain that led to his death so that I could have this new life. Initially, it was hard to give up some of the familiar habits and routines that provided enjoyment, even though they contributed to my mess.

Many times during the course of the change, I have thought or said aloud that God doesn't make sense. How can anyone be available to every one of the billions of people who live on this planet, much less become involved in their numerous, intimate needs? Nowhere have I found an answer to that question. All I can say is that every promise made to me in the Bible has been delivered, and I know there are more to come.

Why doesn't everyone get a visit like mine from Jesus and the Spirit of God? I have met a lot of people who have not, including church members; some don't even agree that such a visit is possible. Again, my answer is incomplete because of my limited understanding, but I do have my own experience as evidence that it happens. Conversations with other men and women help me realize I am not unique in having a personal encounter with Jesus. In fact, the Bible itself extends an invitation to do so to every one of us—and God is in fact there.

Along with my natural human pride, I grew too full of the logic of contemporary thinking to be receptive to the unexplainable mystery of God. The miracles of technology and science bewitched me into thinking that we, as human beings, were the creators. This left little room to notice or receive the One who works first in the heart.

As I listen to other people, I realize these obstacles are common to most of us and partially explain why people facing physical, emotional, or spiritual crises are often able to claim such an encounter with God. When we arrive at a time when it is obvious that we are not in control—that the things or people we believe in, including ourselves, either prove inadequate or completely fail us and we have nothing left to hope in, we become desperate, agonizingly aware of our hollow belief structures. At such times we are more willing to ask if there is more—if there is something to this God story.

Does that mean God will come to us only when we are crumpled in defeat? No, as Jesus demonstrated many times when healing someone, all that is needed is belief in God. Most of us find it harder to retain our hard walls of resistance during times of crisis. Opening them to God every day of our lives, both good days and bad, is the essential key to accessing this new life. Things started to happen after I took that step.

If you are completely satisfied with yourself and your life, then you don't want to meet Jesus. Jesus is change. In spite of my inability to recognize my need, change was what I wanted—and it's what I received.

Is it necessary to have an easily stimulated imagination such as mine to meet Jesus and know God? No. Jesus uses music, dance, nature, science, friends, strangers, poetry, crafts, late night walks, or any number of other circumstances to speak to us. God is creative and uniquely available to us in all things and places, as well as in each other. Once that relationship blooms, God can even use each of us to be the means by which he is seen or heard in someone else's life.

As I reflect for a moment on all that has taken place, I notice movement in the mirror again.

I see Jesus looking back at me now, again appearing as Poortvleit would paint him. His smile holds all I have been given—the acceptance, the love, the cleaning, and the renewed life and sense of purpose. It has been reflected onto me from him, like it had been with those men and women whose stories I read, and now I can reflect it onto someone else. What a responsibility! What an opportunity!

What about the Mad Parade then? Does it still beat its way outside this sparkling place of peace? Yes, because it represents life, where everything good and everything bad meets. However it will no longer dominate me or force me to march to its tune. It has been unmasked.

The sanctuary of the renovated Boarding House and it's number one boarder, the Holy Spirit, will continue to refresh God's will in my life as I move through the parade with confidence and purpose, safe in the knowledge of God's presence, forgiveness and love. I draw in another deep, long look into those joyful eyes in the mirror, as it becomes my own image again.

I'm not perfect or complete but I have a new life.

Another renovation by the Carpenter of the New Testament.

You have turned my mourning into joyful dancing.
You have taken away my clothes of mourning and clothed me with joy,
that I might sing praises to you and not be silent.
O LORD my God, I will give you thanks forever!

Psalm 30:11-12